DATE DUE

Grapes
of Conflict

Grapes of Conflict

by

SYDNEY D. SMITH

foreword by

CESAR CHAVEZ

HOPE
Publishing House
Pasadena, California

Copyright © 1987 by
Hope Publishing House
P.O. Box 60008
Pasadena CA 91106

Manuscript editor: Faith Annette Sand

Library of Congress Cataloging-in-Publication Data

Smith, Sydney D., 1915-
    Grapes of conflict.

    1. Church work with migrant labor—United States—
History.   2. National Farm Worker Ministry (U.S.)
3. United Farm Workers Organizing Committee.   I. Title.
BV2695.M5S65 1987   261.8'34563   86-27754
ISBN 0-932727-12-3
ISBN 0-932727-13-1 (Special ed.)
ISBN 0-932727-14-X (pbk.)

To Evelyn

A great woman who shared the adventure of my life and joined with her whole heart in the quest for justice for farm workers. Her faith, love, wisdom, wit and courage sustained us throughout our joyous life together.

Contents

Foreword

I'm sure that the relationship that we had with the migrant movement is unique in the history of the labor movement—perhaps it is unique in the history of social movements in our country.

Obviously the churches have been close to labor's struggles and have supported the cause of labor in many times and places during the past 100 years. But in this instance, one specific arm of the church—the Migrant Ministry—stood with us, picketed with us, marched with us, *lived with us* from the first days of our strike in Delano until the battle was won.

They not only collected food for the strikers and told the rest of the world about our struggle—they sent their staff to be with us, 24 hours a day. In time our case became the heart of their mission—despite the fact that the organized wealth and power of the rural and conservative churches was trying to put them out of existence.

I don't know in detail all the pressures that Chris Hartmire and Jim Drake were under in those early years of the Delano strike. I do know they were enormous; to many leaders they would have been overwhelming. Somehow Chris and Jim managed to handle the raging controversy within the church and still organize the support we needed in the strike and the boycott. It is one of the key reasons why our movement survived.

The Migrant Ministry is central to the farm workers' struggle for justice and central to the improvements that farm workers and their children have experienced over these past 20 years.

It is a great story in the history of labor and in the history of the church. Syd Smith, who was himself one of the key figures in this story, has done a service for us all by analyzing and recording these events. To my knowledge, it is the first time it has been done and I recommend Syd's book to all those who yearn for justice in our land.

—**Cesar Chavez**

Introduction

Reading Sydney Smith's good book brings back a flood of memories. I remember the opposition and the conflicts well. But these are less memorable than the amazing stories of the U.F.W. strikers and boycotters—men, women and children who had never had a practical way of fighting back against their exploiters but who were transformed by a new energy and a new hope. Cesar and Dolores and the other leaders of the union had found a way to fight, without violence, and to win! The workers who followed that nonviolent way were changed forever.

Farm workers made sacrifices for their union which, in retrospect, are hard to believe. They marched, sang, picketed, organized, went to jail, fasted and traveled to strange and distant cities for their cause. They shared their lives and their hopes with anyone who was willing to walk with them for even a short part of their journey.

We in the Migrant Ministry were fortunate to be as close as we were. The hard things we did never seemed that hard because we were part of this great change surging through the farm worker community—besides, the people of the union were doing even harder things.

The church leaders who supported us in those days had a tougher time of it. They had more than their share of the conflict but they only occasionaly experienced the hope filled, energizing spirit of the workers and their movement. They were deprived of much of the positive juice that kept us going day after day.

Cesar and I met along the way. We are different in many ways. He was clearly the strong leader of this movement while I was one part of the union's support network. Our relationship developed primarily because the union had urgent needs and we in the Migrant Ministry responded. Cesar came to trust that we would help whenever we could and without expecting anything in return. Friendships forged in the midst of crisis and struggle tend to be tight and longlasting.

I would like to take this opportunity to identify the Migrant Ministry staff who lived through those tumultuous years immediately following the 1965 Delano grape strike, especially those not named in this book: Mary McFarland, Lupe and Kathy Murgia, Jan and Dale Van Pelt, Dick and Ann Sample, Suzanne Havens, Sandy Clark Sample, Carol and Phil Farnham, Russ and Peggy Paulson and Gene and Luana Boutilier. I would also like to say "thank you" publicly to my wife Jane and our four children—John, Janie, David and Gordon—for their love and patience during those ever changing, pressure packed years.

Syd Smith's book is clearly a labor of love, generated by his own deep faith and his involvement with the farm about justice for farm workers and especially to those who seek to unite the community of faith with the struggles of the poor.

—**Wayne C. "Chris" Hartmire**

1. Getting Involved

From time to time there comes upon the cool, calm waters of life in the church a ruffling disturbance not unlike that at the sheep pool. The trick for observers is to determine its source—angel of the Lord or ornery human ego? Often when severe strife arises in the church, the root of the conflict is found in differing human concepts of mission strategy and action.

A major event of this kind occurred in the 1960s when the California Migrant Ministry—a small, ecumenical body of the Protestant churches—responded in faith, with a radical but theologically orthodox action, to injustice being visited upon seasonal farm workers. The Migrant Ministry exemplified one clear, theologically authentic approach to the needs of a specific group of oppressed poor persons, but it was in no way a conventional response.

To put this story in context, perhaps I should sketch out a bit of my personal background and the stimuli that led to writing this book. Tracing the route, one naturally wonders how an ordinary, middle class person could be involved in the controversial and prickly issue of ministry with farm labor, let alone help a farm labor union organize.

I had the good sense to be born in Los Angeles—at a time when it was smog-free and relatively unsophisticated. My parents were kindly, compassionate and concerned persons but not at all religious. My only exposure to the church before reaching mid-life was as captain of a local YMCA basketball team which played in various church gyms—an activity of minimal theological significance.

Dad, brought up in New England, was the son of a minister.

Genteel poverty would best describe the economic situation of his family. Apparently their observance of the proverbial blue laws and strict Methodist doctrines restricted him too much, so he came West in his early teens and had no relationship with the church for the remaining 70 years of his life.

The contrast between his father, a scholarly but impoverished minister, and his uncle, a prosperous Beacon Hill physician, influenced Dad to choose medicine for his career. He came alone to California where he graduated from Los Angeles High School and then attended the University of Southern California, making enough money playing the flute in the Los Angeles Symphony and at Levy's Restaurant to pay his way through school. After graduating from Stanford University, Phi Beta Kappa, he went on to Harvard Medical School, finishing Summa Cum Laude. Along the way he managed to marry my mother, the only daughter of a wealthy mortgage banker.

That gave to me an interesting and rather privileged childhood filled with good times, many friends and family outings. Our summers were spent at the beach in La Jolla or Coronado. If anyone got very serious about life, it didn't last long.

The combination of an overachieving father and an escapist, charming mother tended to make me a dilettante. My sporadic schooling included periods at Pomona College, USC, UCLA and the University of London. I pursued what might be called "self-study" under various guises during several years of world travel. I liked to call it "applied sociology" but other names, such as dropout, might be more accurate. I did manage to explore many aspects of world cultures. My education followed random rather than sequential learning patterns which some say is how learning naturally occurs. I never returned to formal academic life.

My world travels derived from my mother who at age 50 decided she should retire. What she retired from escapes me, but the whole family accompanied her into retirement starting off with a trip to the South Seas. During our peregrinations over the next few years my three sisters married while en route—in New Zealand, France and Australia—demonstrating one advantage of travel. Thus our parents, in order to visit their daughters and their families, kept traveling until they were well into their 80s. I finally found my way home, where I made a few more halfhearted attempts at schooling, which was a tedious project after three years and some 100,000 miles of travel on land and sea.

It was then Uncle Sam invited me to join his Air Force. I was drafted and spent the next five years successfully avoiding combat. During this stint, in 1942 to be exact, my wife Evelyn and I were married. I had searched the world over but had found the right person for me back in California. We were married when I received a promotion to the exalted rank of corporal, with a salary of $66 monthly.

During those turbulent war years I had the rather unglamorous role of Food Service Supervisor but managed eventually to achieve the rank of captain. The work was interesting and it helped me avoid overseas duty, for which I am grateful. For ten years after my discharge I achieved modest business success as a dealer-distributor of mobile homes. At the end of this period when I found myself increasingly bored with the money chase, the Holy Spirit took me in hand. I was baptized into the Presbyterian church.

In the military I had learned never to volunteer, yet I did so now to help the church complete a building program which was faltering because the business manager was dying of cancer. When he died a few months later I was offered his position and accepted. Thus, with no previous experience nor apparent qualifications, my ecclesiastical career was launched.

To compensate for my total lack of knowledge of Christianity, Evelyn and I set ourselves to learning as much as possible about the doctrines and the mission of the church. We bought all twelve volumes of the *Interpreter's Bible* and began reading it to each other book by book. New concepts and insights opened for us and enhanced the enjoyment of my work. Our experience in the church was quite different from anything I had known before.

On our first vacation from this church job Evelyn and I visited many sites of the California Migrant Ministry, then a program of the National Council of Churches. At various labor camps, we met the staff and observed their efforts to alleviate the struggles of seasonal, migrant farm workers. More importantly, we saw firsthand the incredibly depressing plight of the farm workers themselves. The fortitude they demonstrated in their lives plus their strong family bonds and the creativity and caring with which they faced their poverty and hard work made deep impressions upon us—from our advantaged position.

Unable to take lightly what we had seen and experienced we arranged for our church school to use a two-week special Migrant Ministry curriculum. The whole church participated. Rev. Douglas Still, the Migrant Ministry Director, occupied the pulpit one Sunday, followed on the next by Dr. Forrest Weir, executive secretary of the Council of Churches in Southern California. Migrant Ministry staff along with the regular teachers taught the curriculum at all grades.

Because of my interest in the farm workers I was appointed in 1958 as an at-large Presbyterian church representative to the California Migrant Ministry state commission. This statewide coordinating and policy setting body had recently been created by the Northern and Southern California Councils of Churches to oversee their ministry with seasonal farm workers. This action followed National Council of Churches existing policy seeking to transfer to local councils more direct oversight and funding of state migrant ministries.

From the time of my appointment in 1958 until 1972, when the National Farm Worker Ministry was formed, I volunteered much time to the leadership of the commission, holding various offices over those years. I was active as an interpreter of this ministry in many churches including those which I served in a staff capacity. We raised money, got food and volunteers for the union, and watched the farm worker movement grow to be a nationwide effort of mainline Protestant churches. Long ago I came to the conclusion that controversy emerges wherever church persons respond faithfully to the cry of the people.

In September 1961 Rev. Wayne C. "Chris" Hartmire became director of the California Migrant Ministry and under his administration the thrust of a new ministry directed toward community organization, begun by Doug Still, was expanded. This gave the church the unique opportunity to fulfill its servant ministry with farm workers, because they alone were determined qualified to set the agenda. But an alliance was thus formed between farm workers and those of us from the middle class churches who found it a new experience to accept our support role and be part of their movement—putting our lives and resources at their disposal.

Together we lived through many exciting events. Our deep commitment to farm workers found expression through the California Migrant Ministry which grew to become the most meaningful aspect of our Christian life. Our becoming intimately involved in the evolution and mission of this ministry gave us an experience of Christian mission in a vital and authentic form.

This farm worker movement, led by Cesar Chavez, also taught us how to focus our lives on a single people, a single struggle. Of necessity we had to let go of many peripheral relationships and otherwise meaningful projects. In the Migrant Ministry we joined our hopes and deeds with those of the farm workers' union as it came into being. Our staff worked side by side with the union staff and we took our goals from the union's goals.

As churches and church people were organized around the needs of the United Farm Workers Union, the strikes, boycotts, prayer services, legislation, marches and celebrations found the two groups thrown together. Most of the church population knew little about the movement. Some who did wished they didn't. A minority cared deeply and contributed sacrificially to those victories achieved by farm workers since 1965 when the Delano grape strike began.

In the light of this background, when I retired from a difficult ten-year stint directing a community based housing services corporation in Pasadena, Chris Hartmire, constrained to keep me from enjoying any idleness, persuaded me to take on the task of writing this history.

Once an interviewer asked Cesar Chavez what he would advise young people to do with their lives. He responded, "I would ask them to choose one important area of human need and focus their energies in that direction so much so that their lives are touched and changed by the people they work with."

As one touched and changed by working with Chavez and farm workers I can testify to the wisdom of Cesar's reply. In this spirit I offer this account of the relationships between the faith community and farm workers, in many of which I was a participant, hoping that others will catch the vision of the gospel promise, "If you give your life away, you will discover authentic life, as God intended it to be" (Mk 8:35).

2. The Alliance Emerges

In the 1960s people from two social classes in America came together with a common purpose. A few middle class mainline Protestants allied themselves with some California farm workers from the lowest end of the economic scale who were determined to create a union. The mainline Protestant churches were represented by an agency of the National Council of Churches, the California Migrant Ministry.

These two disparate groups of people joined hands and hearts in a dedicated struggle to change the status quo. The farm worker leadership was strongly religious, and mostly Roman Catholic. The church leadership tended to be well educated, middle class clergy and laity. This unique alliance between persons of two faith communities and two economic classes was destined, through their struggles together, to produce major changes in both church and society.

How this alliance came about is largely untold history and we need to examine its meaning for today. From 1958 to 1972, as part of the leadership of the California Migrant Ministry, I participated in developing this partnership between the church and the farm worker movement. Added to my own perceptions were those of over 30 others who had participated in these historical events whom I interviewed. Each of them told vivid and individual accounts of their experiences.

This history records how the faith community was strengthened in its commitment to address the unjust conditions of the powerless. Without understanding the full implications, most of these participants from the life of the church, found themselves involved in a significant moment in history.

Remembering these deeds encourages all of us in the church to continue to be engaged in the struggles of all in our society who are oppressed. Christians are mandated by God and the scriptures to seek justice and dignity for all, and to create and maintain just social structures.

Eight assumptions underlie this study:

1). Power in Society.

A power struggle lies at the core of the farm worker movement. The dynamics of power in society need to be understood by the participants of such an alliance in order for a movement to be effective. The disparity between agribusiness power and farm worker power is clearly the context of their oppression and resultant struggle. Justice for farm workers requires realignment of this power imbalance. An adjustment favoring workers would eventually bring about a greater measure of equality.

2). Cooperation between Classes.

A spiritual, pragmatic, cooperative and institutional linkage was created by the servanthood role assumed by the California Migrant Ministry. This alliance was a distinctly Christian enterprise which crossed class lines, for middle class persons found themselves cooperating, at some risk, with lower class persons seeking liberation. Members of the power*ful* middle class institution, the church, were allied with the power*less* farm worker movement. This close working relationship, in addition to morale-building, gave the farm worker movement access to people, funds and influence in the churches. In spite of strong, active opposition this alliance persisted and grew.

3). Leadership Relationships.

The relationship between Cesar Chavez, the farm workers' leader, and Chris Hartmire, the director of the California Migrant Ministry, developed as a catalytic and creative force in this alliance. The enduring and deep relationship of these two people provided dynamic motive force energizing the church and the union and cementing the alliance. Examining their lives we find that they both developed specific character traits, life experiences, training, spirituality and a keen sociological awareness. Hopefully, this study will provide some insights which will help identify leaders in church and community for future justice ministries.

4). The Church in Society.

The leadership of the California Migrant Ministry embraced a specific, particular understanding of the role of the church in society which demanded of all an understanding of active, shared suffering with the oppressed. Although Biblically and theologically well grounded, this view lacked widespread acceptance among church members. In fact its implementation caused great and deeply felt division in the church. Examining this division we find insights for the strategy and methodology of the mission enterprise.

5). Movements of Rising Expectations.

The social ferment of the civil rights movement created a climate of hope and courage for poor and oppressed persons. As they sought justice and recognition of their human dignity, an increase of public awareness of injustice was created. Many persons who might not otherwise have done so were sensitized and responded to the farm worker movement.

6). Nonviolent Resistance—A Tool for Change.

Cesar Chavez' deep commitment to nonviolence to a large degree determined the ultimate success of the movement. By showing a remarkable ability to communicate this stance to followers and by refusing to use violence, even in reaction to violent attacks, he gave the movement great moral strength. Nonviolence as a way of life formed an integral part of Cesar Chavez' vision of agricultural labor relations. Justice both for workers and their employers formed its basic premise. Chavez' nonviolent resistance ethic sought to change rather than overcome the adversary. The farm workers' vision and operational standards thus clearly conform to the church's goal of peaceful change.

7). Subsistence Life-style.

When Chavez and members of the union adopted a life-style of bare subsistence they created a powerful witness to their deep commitment to the cause. Living austerely helped to focus their lives on the essentials—the achievement of their goals. Their meager life-style further figured importantly in attracting many persons to join in the struggle and tended to authenticate the movement and Chavez' leadership of it.

8). Theological Parallels.

The California Migrant Ministry, in its alliance with farm workers, developed a theology of mission through a process of action followed by theological reflection. The specific procedures followed in this development and the resulting theology will be seen to contain striking parallels, as well as major differences, with Latin American Liberation Theology.

3. The Church Community Awakens

One intense evening in 1965 as Chris Hartmire explained the situation farm workers had to endure to a church study group at All Saints Episcopal Church, Pasadena, California, he was asked if he was biased.

His answer explained why he felt the church should be involved in the farm worker situation. "Yes, I am biased towards them because I see farm workers as the most oppressed and also the most essential among workers in America yet they have the poorest health and receive the least health care. They have the least education and their children are exposed to the poorest, often the shortest, educational experience. These serious conditions are partly the result of their migrancy, but they also are the result of racial and class discrimination. Of course all this deeply affects their feelings of self-worth and dignity."

Diversity characterized this church group listening to Hartmire. Mostly affluent, some of them had financial ties to agribusiness, others were ardent supporters of the striking farm workers. They had come together to study the nascent grape strike in Delano, California as the church struggled whether or not officially to support the Migrant Ministry. Discussing the issues uncovered strong feelings, yet the rector, Dr. George F. Regas, and church officers decided it was important to face them squarely in order to reach a faithful Christian response.

And so Hartmire continued to explain how the farm workers received the lowest wages often for the most dangerous physical labor with no protection by the national labor laws and regulations which covered most American workers. Not only did they have to compete with other Americans for this scarce, seasonal work, but they also competed with immigrant workers—legal and illegal—from Mexico and other Third World countries. These factors contributed to their depressed wages because they provided a large pool of docile young men and women willing to work for low wages, usually under substandard conditions.

For these reasons, Hartmire concluded, as a Christian, he was obligated to be biased in favor of farm workers. His explanation of the Migrant Ministry's position challenged many of the theological and sociological assumptions of the group who had not thought much about the farm workers who were disorganized, weak and poverty-stricken while their employers were highly organized, affluent and powerful. This radical power imbalance was the context of the injustice experienced by seasonal farm workers. Since justice demands a countervailing power, Hartmire was convinced this would come as workers organized and had the right to bargain on issues that directly affected their lives.

In the early days of the strike the Migrant Ministry Commission drafted a position paper which was adopted as policy by the California Council of Churches. Basically, it stated that Christians who are identified in Christ with the suffering of their fellows are under biblical injunction to establish justice wherever people are oppressed. Thus the churches in California, working through the Migrant Ministry, had been active in farm labor communities for decades.

However, a parallel observation realized that the mainline Protestant denominations represent the established power order, so from the farm worker point of view, they are among those who deal callously with those who work in the fields. Effective proclamation of the gospel in this situation requires an identification with the farm worker struggle for dignity and purpose.

At All Saints, before this particular six-week study ended, almost 100 persons had heard not only Hartmire, but also diverse opinions expressed by a grape grower, a journalist, a food machinery manufacturer, a rural health worker and a member of the budding farm worker union. Tempers flared, arguments broke out. Discussion settled some issues but not others. Some questions found answers, others remained unresolved. Some minds were changed, but all participants had an opportunity to hear new information and reach new understanding.

This was typical of many churches in the area who faced the specific, immediate issue of economic and social justice for farm workers. Many church groups faced at this time their prejudice, trying to overcome it while arriving at a faithful answer to the farm workers' request for solidarity and support. Soon churches, in order to see for themselves, began to send ten or 20 of their number to spend a weekend in Delano, the site of the strike.

Often such a group would spend some twelve hours with the growers, hearing their point of view, and then move on to meet with the farm workers at their new union headquarters, Forty Acres, listening to their stories for another twelve hours. In this way the church groups could also observe the emerging union at work in its service center, its cooperative service station and its health center housed in a mobile home, but boasting only basic equipment used by its staff—one volunteer doctor and one nurse.

It was normal for such a group to meet and talk with Cesar Chavez, then the president of the National Farm Worker Association (N.F.W.A.). They also visited ranches of Delano growers who were being struck and picketed by workers.

When the All Saints group of 25 returned home from such an excursion, they made a complete report of their firsthand experiences at the next meeting of the full group. One member showed the group a union poster depicting an emaciated little girl and said, "This is obviously a fake and shows what a slanted story the union is trying to foist on a gullible public and a sentimental church."

Dr. David Blankenhorn, a noted cardiologist who had joined those visiting Delano, differed with this opinion for he personally had found a number of malnourished children like the girl pictured on the poster. His examinations confirmed to his satisfaction the authenticity of the poster's message. This diverse response was typical and illustrates the difficulties people of differing points of view face as they search for facts in emotionally charged social situations.

Because of inner tensions and other priorities this particular church was unable then to resolve the issue. It continued its study and debate and some officers further visited Delano. Finally, two years later, the church board took an official position supporting the Migrant Ministry and its work with the Farm Workers Union. A number of church members volunteered for service in the farm worker movement. Testimony based on their firsthand experiences played a large part in the church's ultimate decision to support the Migrant Ministry in its stand.

Often such an action/reflection method is successful in helping people understand social issues. As church members directly confront injustice they gain new, sometimes radical, insights. This procedure is an authentic way to analyze issues for prospective mission action and church resource deployment.

Christians are faithful to their vocation when they act in solidarity with the poor. Thoughtful Christians must try to understand and feel the full dimensions of pain and suffering of their neighbors. Whatever subsequent actions they decide on should then be consistent with this firsthand knowledge and sharing of suffering. Christian social change action is authentic to the degree to which it results from theological reflection based on such direct experience of injustice.

To review the historic involvement of the churches with farm labor issues we must go back further than 1965. Christian concern for seasonal farm labor in the United States was expressed as early as 1920. Over the next 50 years it evolved in three distinct phases: *service—advocacy—servanthood*.

For its first 20 or so years the ministry provided direct services to meet the felt human needs of the migrants. This was a phase of *service*.

The 1940s saw the emergence, as a major strategy, of efforts to pass new legislation and to reform the regulations affecting farm labor. This second phase of the Migrant Ministry, *advocacy*, often dealt extensively with these needs. This church action achieved some notable changes, including the repeal of the *bracero* program in the 1960s. (*Braceros* became the lingua franca for farm laborers employed under contracts with growers that mandated strict standards at prevailing wages, which were negotiated in accordance with Public Law #78, based on a treaty between Mexico and the United States.)

In spite of these improvements the basic conditions of farm workers remained unchanged. By the late 1950s the churches, dedicated to serving the needs of migrant workers, realized that fundamental change in farm workers' lives could occur only through self-determination. The workers themselves would have to gain at least some increase in strength to correct the power balance so heavily weighted in favor of the growers.

And so *servanthood* became the next phase as the churches expressed their commitment to self-determination by workers. Soon servanthood became the primary goal of the Migrant Ministry. This new phase of ministry was propitiously timed as the workers themselves had begun to organize for change and they welcomed a full, committed alliance with the church. Thus a small ecumenical agency, the Migrant Ministry, was ready and able to be the catalyst for this alliance.

One of the first formal ministries to seasonal farm labor started in 1920 when Lila Bell Acheson and others of the Council of Women for Home Missions began a ministry among children of Italian and Polish farm workers who lived in shacks on vegetable farms in New Jersey, Delaware and Maryland. These compassionate women established and staffed four day-care centers for the workers' younger children since the older children worked in the fields to augment family income. Even with the earnings of the older children, wages paid by the growers were barely sufficient to maintain a family at subsistence levels.

Employers provided housing, which amounted to a few shacks with four walls and leaky roof. Without inside running water or sanitary facilities these old dilapidated buildings lacked maintenance, government standards and supervision. As human habitations they could only be described as degrading and clearly constituted health and safety hazards.

In those early days the growers, canners and community

leaders welcomed this *service* ministry, primarily because they perceived the work force as more stable and settled when such services were available. Even though some growers also appreciated the need for education of their workers they made very little effort to provide education for migrants within the regular school systems.

Blanche and Ted Schmidt, church leaders from Dos Palos, California, in remembering this early period, felt there was a marked difference during this early period from what later became the norm. Growers then felt it was in their best interests to have nurses come to the camps to prevent epidemics and promote worker health.

The widespread destructive effects of migrancy include illiteracy, poor health and the necessity to accept very dangerous work at very low wages and under oppressive conditions. Farm workers often put up with a "take it or leave it" attitude by employers. In those days the Migrant Ministry personnel clearly witnessed these conditions but were unable to effect change.

By 1926, growing out of this early work, the National Migrant Ministry was created although it continued to be related to the Council of Women for Home Missions. Edith Lowry had joined the Migrant Ministry staff that year and became its national director in 1928. She guided the Migrant Ministry with distinction until her retirement in 1962. Its staff included teachers, nurses and other people with caring skills. Eva Barnes, a nurse from the Presbyterian Church, USA, had health work going in 23 camps in California by 1928.

Soon this compassionate work was operating in 15 states offering services which ranged from child care, recreational activities, vocational training, literacy classes, English studies, religious services and referral to health, welfare and educational resources in the community. A dedicated corps of missionary nurses, community workers and volunteers took part in this program.

The Migrant Ministers used station wagons and cars they named "Harvesters"—carrying the identifying seal of the National Migrant Ministry on the door. Each Harvester was equipped with a public address system, a film projector and screen, some first-aid supplies, recreational gear, a chaplain's folding altar and a field organ.

Through a major funding campaign in 1945 the Ministry obtained a fleet of these vehicles. As they moved throughout rural communities—to churches, camps or welfare offices—they became symbols of the Migrant Ministry, creating a visible witness of the churches' caring. Later, in the early 1960s the United Church Women of Southern California, inspired by their president, Ruth Schrader, collected thousands of "Blue Chip" coupon books to purchase additional "Harvesters" for the California Migrant Ministry. For these women "Blue Chip Day" became a modern counterpart of the quilting bee and for the church the farm laborers working in the next valley became a mission field.

4. From Service to Servanthood

During the 1940s the Migrant Ministry staff became increasingly aware that a different approach which would lead to meaningful improvement in the status of farm labor was called for. Although the need for direct social services was far from diminished, the concepts of *advocacy* and *servanthood* arose as a result of growing awareness among staff and lay leaders of the root causes of the migrant workers' problems. This would not have occurred had the staff not been working alongside the farm workers.

So more and more the Ministry staff began to speak out and take public positions on issues of importance to farm workers. As advocates they were often, though not always, supported in this role by local clergy and churches. Some churches in rural locations had difficulty accepting the concept of a church advocating social change and sometimes such action caused sharp divisions within congregations.

David Sholen, a Presbyterian minister from Tucson, Arizona was an early and courageous defender of the migrants. Shortly after World War II he became involved with the migrant problem simply because it was brought to his attention that they did not have enough to eat. When he and some of his congregation tried to see if they could do something about the poor wages and the despicable housing of the farm workers they found themselves facing opposition which arose from their public actions and appeals for justice. Sholen soon realized he was the pastor of a church which did not really want to deal with things like this and many did not want the church members going to the legislature or talking to subcommittees and growers, raising hackles and messing around with what was perceived as non-church business.

In the face of such hostility received from various sources, the Migrant Ministers continued to advocate specific action for change. The several social justice issues they focused on included reducing child labor in the fields, setting a minimum wage for farm workers, providing sanitary facilities in the fields and camps, and observing health laws and housing codes. Minimal enforcement of the few laws dealing with these issues was the rule. Growers often were angered by what they termed "these intrusions." Sometimes, when various growers became the specific targets of criticism, they retaliated by refusing the Migrant Ministers' previously honored request for access to the workers. When this happened because of this advocacy activity, farm workers suffered further, for they were denied even the approved services.

In spite of such setbacks the Migrant Ministry policymakers clearly supported staff efforts to get legislative reform. They implemented a program of active advocacy on behalf of farm workers and in many states challenged local, state and federal agencies to administer the laws justly and in a manner which met the legitimate needs of migrants. Unfortunately, many government agencies responded either negatively or apathetically. Growers increased their pressure to maintain absolute control over their workers. At this time racist and elitist attitudes made themselves keenly felt.

One reason for this response comes from a history of conditions making seasonal farm labor easy prey for manipulation and oppression. For more than a hundred years California growers had imported labor. No precedent of concern for the needs of migrants existed. Since the 1850s domestic farm labor could be kept under control because it was plentiful and hungry. This importation policy gave the grower dominance.

At the urging of the farm lobby in the early 1950s the U.S. permitted increased importation of Mexican farm workers under the provisions of Public Law #78. This law implemented a treaty between the United States and Mexico and provided growers with a large number of contract workers, *braceros*, who were paid prevailing wages, furnished good dormitory-type housing for men only and, in general, treated well. It did not, as predicted, reduce the constant flow of the illegal workers—wetbacks—who with their entire families came across the U.S. borders from Mexico, Latin America, Canada and the Caribbean. Thus low wages and a surplus of workers continued to characterize the agricultural scene, especially in the Southwest.

The Migrant Ministry staff stepped into this very controversial issue to help to explain to church members the many negative features of the bracero program. Their actions were supported when the President's Commission on Migratory Labor issued a report in 1960 which showed the depressing effect of P.L. #78 on farm worker wages, the displacement of domestic workers and the elimination of the possibility of collective bargaining between farm workers and their employers. In addition, many farm worker men who traveled north for work in the United States, were forced to leave their families behind, thus damaging the family social structures in their communities.

The bracero debate raged nationally from 1961 to 1964 with churches playing an active role. The Migrant Ministry staff found itself at the center of the controversy. Under mounting pressure, congress finally refused to extend P.L. #78.

This victory for justice was important to the church not just for the final result but because it helped prepare church leaders for the larger conflict that was to come. Denominational and other church leaders who experienced firsthand the ugly realities of social injustice wielded by giant corporations were quick to see the parallels when conflict over the grape strike reached into the life of the churches in 1965.

During the first half of the 20th century rural interests dominated many state legislatures and consequently the prevailing attitudes of rural society found broad expression in law and regulation. These concerns based on growers self-interest plus a general contempt for the "fruit tramps," formed the context in which farm workers lived. In addition to race, occupation and class prejudice they also suffered from "regulation without representation" and unjust laws.

An example of how the realities of rural institutions deeply affected farm workers' lives can be seen in the U.S. Sugar Act which established guidelines for sugar beet field workers. In order for the workers to complain of subminimum wages, established by the Act, they had to go to the County Agricultural Stabilization and Conservation Committee for remedial action. This committee, composed of and elected by the growers, not only administered its own price support program, but also policed itself regarding conformity.

Further, agricultural county boards of supervisors, often dominated by growers, were the bodies who employed the sheriffs responsible for fair and reasonable law enforcement. In times of stress—as when workers were picketing a powerful local grower—sheriff deputies often acted to protect grower interests rather than the law. With a grossly slanted interpretation of "harassment" or "unlawful assembly" they would arrest the picketers.

Likewise the county welfare department and the county hospital, both established to serve the needs of the poor, were controlled by boards of supervisors who also appointed the county housing authority which administered the housing for low income persons, including farm workers. Agricultural employers or their business associates usually dominated these agency governing boards. Farm workers tended to experience these agencies as consistently unsympathetic to their needs. A farm worker mother with a very sick infant could easily wait three days to be seen in the county hospital.

The rent strike at the Linnell Public Housing camp, where management raised rents excessively even though no improvements had been made to the facility in over 30 years of operation, is another well-known story.

As Migrant Ministry personnel related directly with the farm workers their interpretation, shared with various churches, conveyed an increasing awareness of the unjust position of farm labor in society. In this way many church members began to gain an understanding of the causal factors in rural economic life which so often denied workers fair wages and the chance of a decent livelihood.

In response, many church folk volunteered with the Migrant Ministry thereby gaining firsthand insights into the powerlessness of the migrant farm workers, their degraded life-style and the refusal of growers to enter into equitable negotiations with them. In time the path to resolution of these issues became more clearly evident to all—farm workers must achieve the power to change basic conditions of their work and life.

Through this experience with farm workers the church learned what the farm worker had known intuitively. Farm workers knew their voices were ignored. Even though the Migrant Ministry at first tried to be their voice and to advocate their cause, their cries usually fell on deaf ears. Agribusiness ignored any calls for change. What reason did they have to negotiate with their workers? Growers had an adequate supply of passive, very poor, very hungry laborers. Why should they not exercise control and maximize stockholders' profit?

Many agribusiness managers treated workers as com- modities—some with paternalism, others with contempt. Pat Hoffman recalls being new in the San Joaquin Valley in 1958 where her husband was pastor of a small congregation. They began working with the Migrant Ministry during that first summer and Pat heard about an old woman who was given just one day's notice to move out of company-owned housing to make room for more needed workers. Naively she called the wife of the ranch superintendant who along with her husband was a member of their church and asked if there was any way some of those in the church could be of help to the old woman as she looked for another place to live. The superintendant's wife told her no help was needed for this happened every year and that Pat should realize that these people are "just fruit tramps."

This tale points out the the difference between agribusiness and the family farm. Where agribusiness is owned usually by a public corporation which tends to employ professional managers whose stated goal is the maximization of profit for their investors and stockholders, on the other hand the family farm is typically operated by its owners, with few employees. Thus in agribusiness human factors are of secondary concern and labor is seen as just another commodity to be purchased at lowest market price. The financial return is, of course, necessary and important to the family farmer, yet there is a personal attachment per se to the growing of food, to the land and to a way of life for the family farmer.

Another differentiation comes from the share of the market each holds. The 1959 Census of Agriculture reported that five percent of California farmers paid 60.2 percent of farm labor wages and that six percent of the farms accounted for 75 percent of the acreage. This typical concentration of financial power by agribusiness increases year by year. And in many ways the small family farm is as oppressed by the agribusiness system as is the farm worker. Often their agricultural operations are but one of many divisions of these agribusiness corporations such as Standard Oil Co. of California whose primary business, of course, is oil exploration and refining, yet who also farmed 218,000 acres in California in the 1950s.

Agribusiness also tends to dominate American agriculture because of the interlocking relations between these food producers and other giant corporations which function in related fields such as distribution, marketing, financing, transportation, research and mechanization equipment. They even exert a strong influence on farm media—print and broadcast. Because of this quasi-monopolistic control, agribusiness employers often hold arbitrary decision-making power over wages and working conditions. They set their own criteria for hiring and firing and find no reason to negotiate with workers' unions or their representatives.

In 1964 the average male farm laborer earned $1,965 and farm family income averaged between $2,500 and $3,000 annually. These statistics reveal the powerlessness and vulnerability of workers who are not responsibly represented, yet agribusiness employment practices vividly demonstrate the basic inequity in the power relationships between employer and worker.

This power differential is particularly exacerbated whenever use of labor contractors is part of the scene. Under this system a labor contractor, rather than a grower, employs the laborers, becoming the legal as well as the operational employer. This further distances the farm worker from the grower who, of course, controls and directs the workers in the fields and receives the major benefits from the work performed. The system is merely a subterfuge to give an oppressive system an illusion of order and stability. In fact, the labor contractor system enables employers cleverly to avoid collective bargaining with their workers.

The inability of workers to deal directly with a grower essentially denies them even slight power over their working life. Further, this system insulates growers from their workers making it easier as employers to ignore the human needs of their workers, treating them rather as machines. Having abundant, cheap and docile labor without responsibility for fair labor standards, the growers have no incentive to develop good labor relations.

Many labor contractors were recruited from among former farm workers so their education and training did not differ from those they employed. The status gained by becoming surrogate employers, achieved by virtue of their control over available jobs, gave these contractors a great sense of power, which unfortunately they often used greedily and ruthlessly over the lives of the workers.

The system also allows the labor contractor to receive an often substantial cut from the aggregate of the workers' wages. Whether from ignorance or greed the business practices of these contractors usually failed to provide protections normally accorded employees, particularly those covered by contracts or labor law. It was common to find such contractors had made wage deductions for social security taxes but then would neither report or pay these taxes to the Internal Revenue Service. As the government had no record of these tax payments—none having been made—workers would be denied earned benefits when they later applied for them upon retirement or disability. By the time these workers realized that they had been cheated, no redress was available.

The Migrant Ministry commission members talked to many such workers who had been subjected to this type of abuse. Workers did not establish relationships of accountability because they seldom signed on with the same contractor for any length of time. They also had little continuity of employment even though a given worker might work most of the year. Then these workers seldom complained to government officials for they felt defenseless as the voiceless outcasts of the society.

On several occasions the commission met in Calexico, California, which is contiguous with Mexicali, Mexico. In 1960 Calexico had a population of 30,000 to Mexicali's 250,000. There is heavy auto and foot traffic which streams across the border as many U.S. citizens of Mexican heritage live in Mexicali but work in the U.S. Besides this, thousands of Mexican citizens daily cross the border to work—legally or illegally—for agribusiness enterprises in the U.S. valleys.

In this manner agribusiness dominates the Imperial and Coachella valleys socially, politically and through land ownership. These two great valleys, irrigated and highly productive, produce a major portion of the U.S.-grown winter vegetables. In spring and summer melons, lettuce and grapes constitute the major crops of these fertile and peaceful appearing valleys—which often have been the scene of bitter and violent farm labor disputes.

As commission members trying to get involved in the farm worker life, we would rise at one in the morning to visit the area adjacent to the U.S.-Mexico border known as "the hole." Here as many as 10,000 people would be milling about, seeking jobs from the hundreds of labor contractors who would be standing by their buses or stake trucks. Armed with a growers' order for workers, each contractor would begin to bargain with the many applicants, usually taking only the youngest or the strongest workers—or a friend or those who offered to pay *mordido*, which literally means "a bite" but which refers to a bribe. Although the Mexican culture tends to accept the *mordido* as an integral part of all transactions, both private and governmental, it is considered a necessary evil, especially when it is exacted in moderation. It is not considered immoral to the same degree as in U.S. culture, but it is illegal under Mexican law, even though tolerated under accepted conditions.

Once hired, workers board buses or trucks for the "day haul" which can be a short distance away but more often as much as 75 miles one way. Contractors' vehicles, typically old and in poor repair, frequently suffer serious accidents and since they normally carry inadequate or no liability insurance there is little recourse for those involved. State or local governmental supervision of safety standards was normally not exercised, so the overloading of these vehicles added to the risk of death or injury.

Labor contractors would also cruise the barrio streets to recruit in the skid rows of urban cities and rural towns—traditional sources of transient and casual labor. Dean Collins recalled how the Stockton police would arrest men on the sidewalk in the barrio and charge them with vagrancy unless they got on the grower's truck as it came slowly down the street, going to the fields and work.

These contractors' vehicles became, in effect, the workers' hiring hall—that essential feature of an organized union relationship with employers. In the case of farm workers, in their powerless, disorganized condition, growers controlled even their hiring hall instead of its being controlled by them in a democratic union.

The essential injustice of the labor contractor system left the farm workers no meaningful relationship with, or recourse against, their true employer—the grower. Besides the frequent denial of social security coverage and worker's compensation insurance, these laborers found that their working conditions, pay rates and any elements of a normal work agreement, were consistently excluded from fair and equal negotiation of such an agreement. Since the actual employers abdicated these responsibilities to a third party, they avoided meaningful relationships with labor. By this device agribusiness' great wealth was amassed on the economically coerced sweat and toil of these human beings—their workers.

Since the labor contractors were usually financially weak and unstable, they lacked accountability to the employees. In effect, through the contractor system, agricultural employers absolved themselves, legally and psychologically, of their normal employer responsibilities. The system worked economically for growers and contractors but failed as a social mechanism of trust, justice and equity for workers.

Agribusiness benefited greatly by this unjust system. Few growers questioned it ethically. It is not surprising that the psychological effects of the farm labor strife of the 1960s were felt by individual growers with sometimes devastating force. Church members who were growers often felt this ethical dilemma even more acutely. Although the church had always been of comfort to them, now a small segment of it—the Migrant Ministry—challenged their way of life. They felt betrayed.

Very few of the growers could see or appreciate the workers' viewpoint, much less accept the church's alliance with their workers. The anger and intractability that growers displayed during the years of strike and boycott in California may reflect a profound anxiety based, at least in part, on deep feelings of guilt.

These conditions forced powerless farm workers to compete in an oversupplied labor market, work seasonally, face race and class prejudice, and to work without contracts, paid vacations, overtime pay or unemployment insurance. They lacked job security and often felt the handicap of a language barrier. It was not surprising when such conditions often produced a low self-esteem and a self-image of inferiority among the workers.

5. The California Migrant Ministry Is Formed

For change to be possible. a sense of hope was needed as well as the possibility for self-determined social change. In the early years the National Migrant Ministry began by giving direct services with children of the farm worker community and later with adults. As the program grew it expanded with active advocacy, turning to legislative action and regulatory reform to end gross discrimination against farm workers. However. existing health, welfare, labor and education laws were addressed with only moderate change.

In the late 1950s the California Migrant Ministry added a third phase to its ministry, perceiving itself in a true *servanthood* relationship with farm workers. This was a natural consequence of the experiences of providing a service and advocacy ministry. The Biblical concept of servanthood, rooted in Isaiah's suffering servant, was developed into a powerfully authentic tool and properly used for the empowerment of poor people.

Such servanthood meant more than a shift in emphasis, for it required radically different goals and methods based on mature theological reflection and insight. An accurate understanding of social forces was needed to inform all strategic plans. This resulted in a degree of commitment beyond a mere individualistic, caring ministry.

As this servanthood ministry grew out of a faithful response to the indigenous farm worker movement, it meant standing in person alongside farm workers in their efforts at self-determination, dignity and self-esteem. This also required changes in our attitudes, direction and program. We had to learn to accept the farm workers' agenda instead of imposing our own on them. Such changes affected everyone—the staff, commission members and the area migrant committees. Eventually the cooperating churches and their agencies found themselves reordering their priorities to accommodate this new reality. But taking the farm worker movement seriously not only brought a change in our commitment of resources, personnel and funds, it also brought controversy.

Since dissatisfaction must occur before change happens, this reorientation of the Migrant Ministry became a public admission that the current methods needed improving. Dean Collins, the Western regional director of the National Migrant Ministry until 1957, commented at the time, "Direct social service to migrants was necessarily ineffective because it was like first aid for a cut when what was needed was to pick up the broken glass."

Concurrently with these program modifications, changes occurred in institutional relationships. The National Migrant Ministry encouraged church councils to create statewide Migrant Ministries. In 1955 Dean Collins held consultations with California denominational leaders and the executives of the two state councils of churches. By December 1957 the councils had ratified a constitution and some bylaws for the statewide ministry. Although the relationship with the National Council of Churches continued, the new structure enabled more direct involvement by the California church denominations and leaders with this new structure—the California Migrant Ministry.

A statewide commission, with each council equally represented, was formed. This body had policy responsibilities as well as oversight of the staff and program. Cooperating denominations appointed members to the commission who in turn worked with the staff to develop this ministry dedicated to servanthood.

This new structure was crucial to the full development of the servanthood ministry because the state's denominational executives now felt closely related to the California program even though it continued to receive strong support from the National Council of Churches. Two national staff members, Jon Regier of the Division of Home Missions, and William Scholes, the Western Regional Director, kept constantly in touch with

California developments. Scholes even attended most commission meetings. Input and encouragement from these two colleagues guided and facilitated the process of change in many valuable ways.

The changing forms of ministry evolved slowly in response to ever new developments rather than just from isolated events. Conscious, creative planning went into developing the new servanthood ministry. A burst of new ideas were put forth as major new programs were devised to address the difficult problems facing farm workers.

Most important among these creative programs were:

1). The Rural Fringe Ministry, developed in cooperation with major denominations by Douglas Still,

2). The training of the Migrant Ministry staff for community organization ministry, and

3). The implementation of the farm worker-minister concept.

Douglas Still knew that an effective Rural Fringe Ministry required a staff trained and skilled in facilitating the organizing efforts of low income people. While he worked with staff people to develop denominational projects, he and Dean Collins worked together to create such a training plan.

Dean Collins selected for this purpose the Industrial Areas Foundation of Chicago, founded by Saul Alinsky whose community organization methods used highly confrontational, often controversial, techniques. For the program Collins obtained funding from the Emil Swartzhaupt Foundation, one of Alinsky's principal funding sources, which helped in planning as well as supporting this program.

One of Alinsky's projects in California, the Community Services Organization (C.S.O.), was selected as the training organization. This grass roots organization of Mexican-Americans in turn chose their two best trainers, Cesar Chavez and Fred Ross, to do the actual training.

The national staff was well aware of these three organizations and their effective work but they knew also what controversy would erupt in the churches regarding the methods used. In the end it was decided that the known effectiveness of these methods outweighed their controversial nature.

The Schwartzhaupt Foundation made a grant of $137,000 in January 1957 for the training of 30 staff persons over a three year period. Important new skills were learned by the trainees who also gained an increased awareness of the migrants' true situation in the society as well as an understanding of the underlying causes of oppression. A tool for liberation was placed in their hands.

The California Migrant Ministry officially named Douglas Still its director in 1957. In this role he began to equip the staff for their future responsibilities in the developing Rural Fringe Ministry. This program of training in community organization, Alinsky-style, afforded most of the trainees a new experience of working intimately together with their trainers. Thus, there was created a personal bond of shared purpose between the C.S.O. trainers, Cesar Chavez and Fred Ross, and the Migrant Ministry leadership.

Later Chris Hartmire, in analyzing this project, said that there was no doubt that the original training project, sponsored by the Schwartzhaupt Foundation, profoundly influenced the direction of the Migrant Ministry, since it not only put the staff in a position to give some leadership in community organization, but it also allowed them throughout the state to be committed to the task of empowering the farm workers and helping them form organizations of their own. Increasingly the Migrant Ministry staff found themselves in conflict with the poverty program planners, particularly as top-heavy county planning committees developed. And in Hartmire's view, it was the C.S.O. training that prepared them for this conflict and gave them the tools they needed to be effective advocates of the migrant farm workers.

When Hartmire first assumed the directorship of the Migrant Ministry in September 1961 he had also commented on the revolutionary impact this training had on the staff. As a result of the training the people in the program learned to empathize with the frustrations of the men and women they were trying to serve. Basically, the training added understanding to their good will. They began to perceive what traditional charity or good will had done, or failed to do, in the past.

The C.S.O. trainers utilized a nontraditional, no classroom process, following a quasi-Socratic method. Each person in training spent at least three months working alongside either Ross or Chavez as they organized in the field for the C.S.O. The trainees learned the process firsthand in a real life situation and this experience helped them to face reality. And out of this hands-on approach the trainees raised many questions for the trainers to deal with at the end of each day.

At three month intervals Saul Alinsky met with trainees and Douglas Still at the Asilomar Conference Center in Pacific Grove, California. These quarterly meetings became a time for very thorough evaluation sessions. The group kept getting larger until all 30 trainees completed the course. Migrant Ministry staff from California, Arizona and other Western states benefited from this creative training method.

As the training progressed the staff increasingly committed itself to the priority concept of helping farm workers organize for self-determination. The state commission, after considerable discussion, reflection and study, also became committed to this new concept.

This did not happen without a few of the members both of the state commission and the staff expressing some skepticism or doubts at first. The Christian press, too, was often critical of Alinsky and his methods. Many church members and leaders distrusted his confrontational and conflictual approach, deeming them inherently unsuited to church work and feeling that reconciliation was the form of ministry more consistently appropriate for the church. The factor they failed to take into consideration was that reconciliation is almost impossible when there is a great power imbalance between the parties. This was certainly the case between employers and their employees.

Great resistance to the more drastic of Alinsky's methods appeared at the denominational level. As the following list shows, however, many of his principles are quite psychologically sound and not all that radical.

The Migrant Ministry staff adopted and promoted the

following ten Alinsky principles for organization:

1). Work *with* rather than *for* people.

2). Work not *just* on a problem, rather get at those people who caused the problem or who can help in its solution.

3). Realize that residents of the community are more concerned with their problems than any outside group.

4). Remember that local persons must do the job and can do it if they are given the opportunity.

5). Be cognizant that the American way of life is to feel you *belong*.

6). Identify the interests which caused the problem and then keep steady pressure on until the problem is solved.

7). To improve one's situation one needs more than just a cause and to get something from one's politician; voting power is needed—which requires a mass-based organization.

8). To develop a mass-based organization among marginal persons one must not only involve their own existing institutions—such as their churches—but also concentrate on "bread and butter" issues and refrain from bringing in other ethnic groups.

9). Achieve some visible success initially and quickly in order to build hope and sustain it.

10). Always remember that effective leaders can be found at all levels of society.

These ten principles, although slightly modified by changing conditions, were effectively used by Chavez and Ross in their work with farm workers in California. Later when Ross was asked to define the kind of person he tried to be as an organizer, he listed the following qualities, abilities and ways of doing things as being very important.

1). The ability to grasp the ideas and aspirations of people and be sensitive to their feelings.

2). Having a constant awareness of and the ability to articulate the concept of "organization" as a frame of reference in all kinds of action.

3). The ability to apply automatically a general know-how of organization to particular problems.

4). The ability to listen and play the role of a sounding board.

5). An ease in relating one's own experiences and attitudes to those of the people.

6). Having qualities such as patience, frankness, obliviousness to the passage of time, tact and a willingness to stay in the background so as to not appear to "hog the show."

These may sound simple, but reflecting on them one can see how essential, even profound, they are.

Two other additional principles came to be stressed:

1). Teaching and learning are best done in the context of action, and

2). Unsophisticated community people will take responsibility, showing growth as leaders, when given the opportunity.

By applying these principles, leaders who have been given new hope and strength are "called out" of the community of marginalized peoples.

Of course the foregoing is merely a brief discussion of community organization techniques—extensive literature on the subject exists—but these are pointis that Chavez, aided by the Migrant Ministry staff, adapted to the particular needs and organizing efforts of the National Farm Workers Association (N.F.W.A.). The staff in the process gained insights and learned to perform a ministry which honored the dignity of the poor, recognized their innate strengths and motivated them to self-determination. In keeping with Alinsky's principles Chavez made certain modifications in his own methods on the basis of the ethnicity and culture of Mexican-Americans and his own insights.

Chavez felt that Alinsky's methods were not fully applicable to their needs on some issues. For example, Alinsky's eighth point required the organizer to involve the community's own existing institutions to build the mass base. Chavez felt that with the lack of existing institutions among the farm workers, he needed to invent usable inst9tions—so he used the house meeting. This was comfortable to rural Hispanics who were used to gatherings in their homes because they had come from areas where there are no public buildings. In a technique developed by Fred Ross, house meetings were used to build this needed mass base. Typically, at such house meetings the hosts would invite a number of friends over to meet with Chavez who could then discuss the plans for organizing with them in a nonthreatening setting.

Alinsky thought Chavez would fail in this because the house meeting was unfamiliar to him. He was wrong.

In 1961 the National Council of Churches Division of Home Missions published.a statement under the title, "National Goals of the Migrant Ministry for the Fifth Decade." Item 9c of the suggestions for implementing these goals came under the heading, "Responsible and Democratic Organization for Economic and Civic Self-help" and stated the following: "State and local Migrant Ministries should vigorously promote the concepts of self-help and self-determination in all their relationships with the community."

When asked to consider this novel directive, the California Migrant Ministry was able to respond saying they knew already that direct services did not bring about significant social change for they had already learned in the fields that mere advocacy, however ardent, often failed even though the cause was just.

Farm workers operated from a base without real power. Unfortunately the church, with its great potential power base, lacked both existing channels and the will to use its power base for the cause of farm workers. The Migrant Ministry program, on the other hand, could provide an effective channel, especially as increasing numbers in the churches became concerned about finding ways to enable farm workers to achieve greater power. Justice would only come when the strong voices of a people on the move would be heard on their own behalf. For these reasons the alliance forged by the Migrant Ministry and Chavez found a vital response from the church of middle class America. At last the voices of the farm workers began to be heard.

Such community organization building on a mass base held great promise for effective social change. Cesar Chavez and a core of colleagues committed themselves to the struggle for "as long as it takes." The Migrant Ministry, recognizing the validity of their cause, made a servanthood commitment to the migrant workers through Chavez and their movement. Such was the dedication of this small group of church folk that they would soon make an impact, disproportionate to their size, upon the whole church.

When the 1960s began, few could see the momentous events which lay ahead. As a new and vital relationship between the religious community and farm workers was forged, the decade brought into being a new spirit of independent action by farm workers. This determined, creative and eventually successful movement achieved increased power for farm workers. They earned a greater measure of justice for themselves and they felt a new sense of strength and dignity in the righteousness of *La Causa* (literally, The Cause, as they called their movement).

Early on, Cesar Chavez publically acknowledged that the participation of the church was crucial to the success of their movement. Under Chavez' guidance farm workers joined the alliance with the church with confidence and dignity. Cesar credits Chris Hartmire as the interpreter and faithful personal friend whose relationship to him and the farm worker movement was an essential factor in building this bridge to the church.

Chavez has also said that in his opinion the church participation in the movement would not have been as effective if Chris had not been there before the struggle started. Chris served as an interpreter who really knew inside and out what the farm worker movement was because he had been there from the start.

As the Migrant Ministry became allied with the farm workers' union it increasingly understood the complex issues involved in its struggle. With more conscious awareness, with study and debate, by the early 1960s the Migrant Ministry had developed a strong theological position undergirding its ministry.

Together with the union, the Migrant Ministry emerged as a major new force for justice in the nation. This growing entity, working for radical social change, created a solid base of people power through the alliance of the faith community with the farm worker community.

Several unique features characterize its nature:

1). The blending of religious and secular institutions in common social change efforts.

2). The bringing together, in shared purpose, a broad alliance of two major economic classes.

3). The combination of high ethical purpose with tough-minded, pragmatic labor union strategy.

6. Organizing a Rural Fringe Ministry

In 1951 when Velma Shotwell (Lerned), Western regional director of the Migrant Ministry, employed Douglas M. Still, a credentialed teacher, she told him to begin a process that would lead to the involvement of school people and schools in a better understanding of the educational needs of migrant children. She also wanted him to try to get the authorities to extend the school programs for migrant children's special needs.

Velma sent Doug and his wife, Hannah, also a credentialed teacher, to Bakersfield, California. They worked diligently to collect important data that substantiated the fact that the family working conditions, in addition to the very fact of their migrancy, negatively affected their children's achievement. Often migrant children lagged one to four years behind their peers.

School officials acknowledged the special educational needs of farm worker children but they remained completely unwilling to extend any special services to migrant children. Still's suggestion that specially designed programs for migrant worker children be developed and implemented met resistance from a school board that reflected the community's bias against farm workers.

The Stills concluded that the schools were not going to deal with the needs of migrant children. In their view the church and its Migrant Ministry must remain steadfast in their commitment to the farm worker children's special needs.

After this direct exposure to the migrants' problems and their life conditions, Still felt the Migrant Ministry needed a fresh approach. Even at this early stage he began to discern the outlines of a new style of ministry. Still envisioned three staff persons—a pastor, a community organizer and a group worker. This team could organize in rural slums among farm workers, seeking justice with a goal of helping these workers deal with issues affecting their lives and work. Such a "rural fringe ministry" would naturally be a cooperative effort of church and farm workers and eventually would lead to an autonomous organization.

Still also realized that in order to have sufficient preparation for developing this church ministry it would be well to have more than a degree in education. He needed ordination and resolved to get it. Enrolling at Union Theological Seminary, New York, Still's course work in practical theology included community organization methods and social group work.

At the end of his middler year at Union, Still returned to the Migrant Ministry to coordinate its summer program. It was then his concepts for a rural fringe ministry crystalized. Dean Collins, who had assumed the directorship from Mrs. Shotwell, accepted his ideas enthusiastically and subsequently hired Still in 1956 to handle the rural fringe ministry (a team ministry organizing farm workers according to their agenda for justice and self determination).

To launch this new ministry Still challenged executives of cooperating denomination's mission boards. Five initially agreed to create such a ministry: the Presbyterian Church, USA; the United Church of Christ; the Methodist Church; the Christian Church (Disciples of Christ) and the Augustana Lutheran Church.

Douglas Still envisioned several functions for the Migrant Ministry in these new relationships with denominations:

1). Educate denominations as to needs.
2). Help denominations initiate projects.
3). Provide consultation regarding mission.
4). Provide staff training.
5). Coordinate projects, and
6). Relate migrants to existing churches.

In a December 1958 report to the executive board of the Division of Home Missions of the National Council, Still outlined his concepts for the rural fringe ministries. These concepts dealt with institutional arrangements, communication between persons of differing social and economic levels, segregation and the need for the ministry to relate fully to farm workers and their families in all aspects of their life and work.

Regarding communication he pointed out, "The failure of rural churches to be missionary is not a theological problem but a socioeconomic problem."

This became a guiding principle for Still in the wider context of the existing social and economic tensions in society. Decent wages and working conditions became a focal point of ministry. This achievement by workers, through self-determination, became the operational goal for the rural fringe ministry.

Within two years Still could report that work was underway in six Central and Southern California rural slums: the Presbyterian Church, USA in Brawley, the United Church of Christ, Congregational, in Bakersfield, the Methodist Church in Corcoran and Mendota, the Augustana Lutheran Church in Lamont and the Christian Church Disciples of Christ in Dos Palos.

Each rural fringe ministry was organized to fit local conditions and meet denominational requirements. Although the various churches defined their denominational projects as to form and strategy, meeting the expressed needs of the people in the chosen location became the primary purpose. Still assisted the churches' planning by raising key questions and providing necessary information about the farm workers, their problems and suggesting possible solutions.

As the projects developed, Still consulted frequently with denominational executives who in turn freely shared their problems and experiences. The staff training conferences became major events for those involved because there developed strong, mutually supportive relationships between the migrant ministry staff and the denominational staff. Through these joint efforts a number of effective ministries developed. They achieved relevance and authentic response to the migrants real needs through the actual involvement of workers in the decision making process.

The Migrant Ministry, in its role of consultation, coordination and overall supervision, served the mission boards well. The participating denominations achieved important goals, not only through the development of the ministries, but also for the success of cooperative events still to come. With a key element—the farm workers' active participation—this ministry in rural communities innovatively dealt with farm labor issues. It was rewarding for all involved to watch the workers, undergirded by these ministries, achieve some modest power over their own lives for the first time.

Gradually there emerged a cross-cultural, inter-class alliance between the faith community and the farm workers. This powerful bond was the result of a ministry characterized by the sharing of power, decision making and a realistic view of society.

In 1957 Still became director of the California Migrant Ministry. He continued the direct services and advocacy phases of ministry in its general program, yet he also worked on new creative ministries. A number of local migrant committees were formed throughout the state to assume responsibility for the work in their own area. Such committees included representatives of local churches and councils of churches. This network of cooperation between local and statewide work enhanced and expanded the ministry to farm workers.

By encouraging self-determination and indigenous organization by farm workers, the rural fringe ministry created new opportunities for them. These new relationships opened the way for the Migrant Ministry to actualize its *servanthood* ministry with farm workers. The evolution from service to servanthood was now complete, yet much experience, action and theological reflection would take place before this servant ministry would assume its full stature. A learning process began for all participants.

Two specific illustrations follow which show how Migrant Ministry and the denominational agencies organized among people with different needs. Both the work done in Dos Palos and in Porterville demonstrate how this more effective approach to social change led to much controversy in the church community.

Dos Palos, California

In this Central California town Douglas Still challenged the Christian Church to develop a community development project in an adjacent rural area. Both the Northern California Conference and the national church executives agreed jointly to sponsor this project. A decision was reached to begin the project in an unincorporated rural fringe slum area, south of the town of Dos Palos, which had some 1,000 black residents.

Two factors made this project auspicious: the Dos Palos Christian Church was blessed with both an active lay leadership and a strong pastor and also the fringe community itself had demonstrated dynamic indigenous leadership which had already coped with many serious community problems.

Years before, black farm workers had settled outside the town in an area with such strongly alkaline soil it held no value for farming. "Good for nothing," it lacked municipal facilities, roads and services. The only water available cost one dollar per month—for this fee a resident received a key with access to a single hydrant at the edge of Dos Palos plus the privilege of toting the water. Such conditions characterized rural slums throughout the California agricultural valleys.

Several lay leaders in the Dos Palos Christian congregation became concerned about the needs of these low income black farm workers. Mr. and Mrs. Ted Schmidt were typical. Both were highly respected leaders in the church and the community. Blanche was an elementary school teacher and principal for over 34 years in the Dos Palos schools while Ted farmed and taught in the high school. Their contribution to the project was strong Christian leadership, courageous and compassionate.

Due to the efforts of a local preacher, a number of the residents in the black community organized and managed to acquire a plot of land which they dreamed of turning into a community center or a park. In anticipation of this they formed a local association the—George Washington Carver Club.

The Dos Palos Christian Church offered to provide this club with the necessary materials and resources for them to build a suitable community building. Upon completion this building would become the property of the Carver Club. Further, they offered to assist in developing a program to be defined by the residents. In addition the church committed itself to provide on-going support to the Carver Club. When the building was completed in the summer of 1959 great joy accompanied the handing over of the keys to the George Washington Carver Club—the new owner.

The Dos Palos Christian congregation decided to embark on this innovative project after considerable internal struggle. For the church to deal with "other persons" in the rural slum offended many members and threatened others. "I don't want any black people coming to *my* church!" was the fear most often voiced. Some in the church opposed any ministry which might result in the eventual "mixing" of races and classes within the congregation. A number of members left the church, others became inactive.

Most of those who stayed accepted the new ministry, although sometimes reluctantly. It was a totally new experience to have the church allying itself with persons oppressed by the socioeconomic system in which most of them found comfort and acceptance. However, being involved in this process, a number of people changed their attitudes from indifference to their neighbors' suffering to active caring about their situation.

Benjamin Fraticelli, the church's pastor, gave psychological and spiritual support to the congregation as they engaged in this transforming process. He encouraged the church members and trained them to participate in this new and difficult social change ministry.

To fulfil the second part of its covenant—assisting in the center's program—the church hired a community worker, Bill Maxon, a white man experienced in agricultural extension. Although he was paid out of the state denominational budget, Maxon reported to a local church committee and worked closely with Pastor Fraticelli who was his supervisor.

The church eventually realized that in employing Maxon it had made a mistake—not because he had not done an adequate job, but because they had misplaced the locus of control in the church rather than the community. Eventually Maxon resigned and a black community resident, Art Jenkins, replaced him.

This time it was the people of the community, rather than the church, who made the decision and chose Jenkins, the town barber. Under his leadership the relationship between the church and the black community changed radically. Now with the indigenous leadership they had chosen, residents felt as if it was their own project and they were more comfortable about participating.

The source of initiative also shifted as Jenkins and the community began to set their own agenda. The Migrant Ministry fully encouraged this transfer of power as a necessary part of the dynamic for authentic social change. Fraticelli and the church members accepted their secondary role—an unaccustomed and new relationship for most white, middle class persons. The church members, as their commitment required, faithfully supported the goals and actions set by the residents according to their own perceived needs.

Tensions however increased between the church and the newly assertive black community, caused mostly by differences of strategy and timing. The church learned through these experiences that social change brings stress and that having differences of opinion is essential in the struggle for justice.

These tensions reached a peak when the black community decided to start a boycott in protest of the discriminatory hiring practices at the local market—their primary source of supplies. Many in the church felt a gradual, negotiated approach without resorting to pressure tactics was preferable to more direct action. Having learned from experience that success was achieved only when they used their collective strength, the black community chose not to count on good will to bring about change.

Further, Fraticelli and Jenkins hoped to establish natural ties between the parish members and the residents of the rural slum. They tried to organize community activities around the common needs of both groups that would become an integral part of the parish ministry.

Working together as a team, Jenkins and Fraticelli tried also to develop a dual approach to community organizing. In addition to each working in their primary area, Fraticelli would also work in the fringe community while Jenkins would work in the church.

In effect they placed an "in" organizer in the "out" group and an "out" organizer in the "in" group in an attempt to create change in both communities. This innovative approach never achieved complete success, but one hopes that it might succeed in other cases under different circumstances.

Fraticelli, an attractive young minister recently graduated from seminary, had tried to establish good rapport with the members of the congregation *before* proceeding to the controversy-producing community development project. Because this initial bond of trust had developed, the Dos Palos Project was as effective as it was. This important factor should be remembered by any who would use this as a model to follow.

Wisely, Fraticelli also avoided some of Saul Alinsky's more confrontational techniques. Instead he applied the Alinsky maxim: "To change an institution change its constituency" by actively recruiting persons outside the church who might be supportive of change. When many of these people joined the church, as new members they developed into a strong support group for the project. With Fraticelli's help this group gained a vision of social justice in an arena of socioeconomic life that they had formerly taken for granted.

The Migrant Ministry staff also worked closely with this alliance between a poor minority community and the church at the local, state and national levels. Blanche Schmidt of the Dos Palos church represented her denomination on the California Migrant Ministry State Commission and kept the commission informed of the progress and problems in this community development project.

Over the next four years members of the Dos Palos Christian Church became involved in various social change projects such as working alongside their allies in the farm worker community, joining in their struggle to obtain a water system for the area or assisting the residents build some self-help housing units. Many even participated in the boycott for fair employment for blacks in the local market, thus displaying an active solidarity with their rural colleagues.

The black farm worker community remained legally separate

from the town of Dos Palos. While they did work on some matters together no real unity existed between the two communities. Eventually the church deeded back the property to the George Washington Carver Center as the two groups drifted apart again.

Together they had won some significant battles for social justice and change, no small accomplishment. As a lasting monument to their efforts, the rural area now enjoys a water system, sewers, a park, paved streets, a county housing authority project as well as self-help housing. Thus, as a result of an alliance between the small but faithful congregation of the Christian Church of Dos Palos and the Migrant Ministry staff, a group of powerless individuals was helped to develop a strong community confident of its own power to make independent decisions and bring about needed social change. Because of this rural fringe ministry these farm workers improved their lives and the future of their community.

Porterville, California

Another example of how the Migrant Ministry related to farm workers can be seen in the story of the Tulare County Community Development Project (T.C.C.D.) in Porterville. What happened here furthered the growth of the alliance between farm workers and the church because it was here that the Migrant Ministry and the farm worker union, headquartered southwest of Porterville in Delano, first joined forces to engage in a struggle for radical, permanent social change.

Prior to this the United Church of Christ (U.C.C.), with the Migrant Ministry participating, had initiated a community development project in the Tulare County community of Goshen. Their goal had been to help the area residents articulate and deal with their problems through their own citizen's organization, which was then located in a community center. The project was led by James Drake with Migrant Ministry direction.

Upon graduation in 1962 from Union Seminary, New York, Drake had first looked for conventional employment in a local parish. Through a friend he met Migrant Ministry Director Chris

Hartmire who offered him the job in Goshen to create and direct the United Church of Christ's first community development project.

Learning from their experience in Goshen, the U.C.C., in 1964 the local church and the national board joined forces with the Migrant Ministry and the Kings-Tulare Migrant Ministry, to sponsor an interchurch committee whose aim was to develop a countywide grass roots effort—which turned out to be the T.C.C.D. project.

The sponsoring committee conceived of its purpose as twofold: 1). To help low income people deal with their own problems in organizations of their own; and 2). To provide continuous interpretation of the needs and actions of the low income people to established citizens (church people and others) so they could understand and respond humanely.

To run the project the committee sought a full-time staff who would be responsible to the director of the Migrant Ministry and yet would be supported jointly. Funding for this project came from the Rosenberg Foundation of San Francisco, the U.C.C.'s Northern California Conference, its Board for Homeland Ministries, as well as the local Porterville Congregational Church.

The committee hired as the principal staff person, James A. Drake, who had proved to be an effective organizer in Goshen. With a mandate to organize the new project, in 1964 he, along with his wife Susan and their two boys, moved to Porterville.

In Goshen Drake and the community center staff had helped the low income residents successfully address local concerns. However when they were confronted with wider economic issues, such as seasonal farm worker wages, they got nowhere. It was felt by the sponsors that they would have a better chance of success by using a county-wide organizing effort. The decision was made to start the planned community development project, the T.C.C.D.

At this time the Kings-Tulare Migrant Ministry also released its director, David Havens, to work with Drake. These two ministers were later joined by Gilbert Padilla, a farm worker who had demonstrated organizing skills. What was to prove a very effective team ministry was now formed Each of the team members brought valuable skills to the project.

Jim Drake grew up in the agricultural town of Thermal, in California's Coachella Valley, where his father, a lay Methodist, taught public school. Out of a conviction that all children deserved to be educated equally, the elder Drake often got into trouble with the school authorities, for he would literally go into the barrios and fields to bring migrant children to school. Once in school, he further irritated his superiors by giving these children special attention and tutoring to help them keep up with the other children.

These efforts on behalf of migrant children made a lasting impression on young Jim who then little realized that he would give a major portion of his life to the farm worker struggles. When Chris Hartmire offered him the position in Goshen, it took him only 15 minutes to accept. He felt as though he was coming home.

David Havens, a minister of the Christian Church, Disciples of Christ, had been director of the Kings-Tulare Migrant Ministry when they released him to work with Drake on the Porterville project. Like Drake he had trained both with Chavez and in several community organizations in Chicago. The task of interpreting their work to the wider community and area churches fell to him. It was not always an easy or pleasant job and often it led to angry confrontations. Because of project needs this interpretive task finally was left to Hartmire.

Gilbert Padilla, the farm worker member of the worker-minister team, came from Hanford, California where in 1962 he had been one of the founders of the farm worker union. Now the Migrant Ministry paid his salary. As a longtime organizer with the Community Services Organization he had developed a sensitivity and knowledge of working with people which would provide the team with unique, essential insights.

This three person team became a crucial link between the emerging farm worker union, the ecumenical church, one of its constituent denominations and a local church. This relationship was a conscious attempt to relate social change ministry directly with local church life. Since the team soon was helping farm workers organize and take community action which would improve their status and enhance their power, it was bound to produce misunderstanding and controversy.

In the summer and fall of 1964 Jim Drake and David Havens organized what they began to call the Farm Workers Oganization (F.W.O.), turning their full energy into building a Mexican-American farm worker self-help group. One of the first things they did was to sponsor a rally welcoming Governor "Pat" Brown who met with the leaders of the F.W.O. to discuss foreign labor, unemployment insurance and other concerns they had. Although some thought that Brown may not have had much previous face-to-face time with left outs such as the farm workers, but through this meetiing he gave their morale a boost by listening to their troubles, shaking their hands and asking them questions. The T.C.C.D. staff was also convinced that this encounter not only made the farm workers stand a bit taller, but it also must have made an impression on the governor which he would not soon forget.

The team's initial organizing effort focused on low income Mexican-Americans in the immediate area, most of whom were seasonal farm workers. Membership in the F.W.O. was limited to farm workers so that middle-class Mexicans and anglos could not join and dominate the organization. Dues were two dollars per month.

Centering his energies in the Porterville area, Drake concentrated on those justice issues which immediately affected farm laborers: wages, housing and county services. In confronting these issues Drake, Padilla and Havens soon were deeply involved community political action. Before long they had registered 1,000 new voters.

The F.W.O. opened a Porterville service office in October of that year where it operated a gas, oil and tire cooperative for its members. But more importantly, Jim and and the staff engaged in casework at the center with many individuals on a wide range of problems including welfare, immigration, wage claims, court appearances, health needs, housing, employment discrimination, excessive interest charges, fraud and similar difficulties.

These activities clearly affected others in the community—like the merchants, government officials, politicians, bankers and the general townsfolk. In such a close-knit rural town which is largely dependant on agriculture, everyone soon knew that the F.W.O. was directly and critically challenging how farm workers were being treated. Heretofore workers had accepted their lot passively. Soon people in the community were heard to murmur that, "Someone must be stirring them up!" It was with little encouragement from the community that the F.W.O. continued its activities.

In March 1965 a flagrant example of illegal, substandard wages ($1.15 per hour) being paid in the sugar beet harvest in the Porterville area was uncovered by the organization. F.W.O. members testified as to these low wages in a public hearing held by U.S. Secretary of Labor Willard Wirtz who responded by ordering vigorous enforcement of the minimum wage for field workers.

Jim Drake remembers that at that time the issue was sugar beet hoeing for a federal minimum wage, the only one then that applied to farm labor any place, was in effect because the contract was federally subsidized. When the team found hundreds of workers who were not receiving minimum wages, they began to take affidavits to a hearing officer who found in favor of the workers, ordering the grower to pay back wages. This was the issue the workers later testified before Secretary Wirtz who in turn upheld the hearing officer.

It was then discovered that the grower was a kingpin in the Porterville Congregational Church. Soon the church council started having night meetings questioning what this migrant program was really about. To try to calm the waters, the conference executive had to come down to interpret to the congregation what the Migrant Ministry was doing.

This sugar beet controversy illustrates well the ethical ambiguity felt by some individuals in the church. When some members, caught up in such injustice, were opposed by others of the same community, their stance created tensions and distrust and potential conflict began to creep into the community. If you were standing outside the community, you might expect the church to applaude Drake's action and join with the farm workers to pressure the grower to pay legal wages. But the observers at the time wondered whether the church was even interested whether its member, the grower who had violated a federal law, was contrite. In fact, many church members began to accusd Jim of "meddling" and rocking the boat needlessly. Turmoil in the church under such circumstances is inevitable.

During the 18 months Drake worked in Goshen helping low income residents develop a community center, he and his wife Susan had developed a relationship of mutual trust with the religious community. At that time they had lived in Porterville where they were well regarded. They were members of the Congregational church, their son Tommy had been baptized there—albeit the first in the church to be baptized in corduroy overalls. During those days most of the church members accepted the Goshen project as worthwhile and necessary for the low income residents' improvement and well-being. However, they failed to anticipate any radical challenge to the basic arrangements of society.

The T.C.C.D. project's focus on social change challenged the thinking of many church members who did not share such an understanding of ministry or envision such a role for the church. In their opinion, for ministers of the church to confront society so directly on justice issues was not acceptable behavior. Many in the church were defensive of the status quo and protective of their own place in it. The stage was set for major turmoil in the church over the issue of justice for farm workers.

Most church members felt uncomfortable when the clergy took a position on economic issues although few members had any idea of the extent of injustice in farm labor relations. Even less could they see the church or themselves, as individuals, being educated about or becoming involved in doing something to correct these conditions.

Although this was happening during the 1960s when TV news broadcasts and newspapers constantly showed the disturbing events of the civil rights movement, still the community did not want to look at their own problems. When ministers, obvious in their backwards collars, began to be prominently pictured in many of these reports, the Christian community began to be disquieted. Controversy raged throughout the country as to the appropriateness of ministerial actions in areas which appeared so far adrift of churchly matters. Many persons in the mainline denominations found this behavior thoroughly disquieting. The Migrant Ministry and its community development projects appeared to some to be just another disturbing aspect of the civil rights confrontations.

Only a small minority in the church supported and understood the theological and historical validity for aggressive social action on behalf of the poor. Denominational executives and the Migrant Ministry Commission stood as bulwarks throughout, giving solid support to the staff. In this crucible of conflict most commission members found themselves increasingly committed to working with farm workers for self-determination regardless of where that might lead or whatever struggles might ensue.

In seeking to discharge their responsibilities the commission members carefully studied the issues involved and tried to share, firsthand, many of the experiences in the daily existence of farm workers. They also took time to reflect theologically on the meaning of these experiences. This helped the commission members to understand intellectually as well as to empathasize emotionally with the feelings and frustrations of these migrant workers. Such insights strengthened them for struggles yet to come.

Many church members labeled the activities of the Tulare County Community Development Project as radical and threatening to their established way of dealing with farm workers. The Goshen project had appeared more remote from their own situation and it did not address as clearly the functional use of power in the community. The T.C.C.D. struggle, however, directly challenged the community mores, prejudices and practices.

Though the church members had at first welcomed the Drakes into their midst, now some people made personal attacks and whispered innuendos against them. Implications of disloyalty and rumors about the T.C.C.D. staff began to circulate. Drake was accused of being a communist and started to receive crank calls.

In contrast with the strong support they received from the minister. James Hazen, the Drakes experienced a growing feeling of estrangement from most of the church members.

It came to a head in October when the council of the Porterville church, as a result of the turmoil over T.C.C.D. program, appointed a committee to carry out a three month investigation of the project. In mid-January when the committee reported its findings, nine members recommended that the church no longer participate in the project and that it be replaced with another program. A minority report by five members, on the other hand, called for "full participation with involvment in decision making." The issue was obviously not settled.

On January 24, 1965, the church held a tense, and at time sacrimonious, congregational meeting. The hall overflowed as many who were not regular in attendance showed up to vote on this explosive issue. Such was the atmosphere of distrust that someone demanded that the ballots, which had been cast secretly, be counted one by one in full view of the meeting.

The completed count showed a vote of 91 to 39 to withdraw approval and financial support from the project. Earlier the church had agreed to raise a special $3,300 towards Drake's salary. This lopsided vote was a blow to the project supporters and reflected middle-class bias at its best. The views of the majority in the congregation can be summed up as follows: All social problems should be solved gradually and cooperatively on the basis of community consensus. Pressure tactics are unchristian. Community leaders can be counted on to do justice without the need for pressure. Our Mexicans are content but the Migrant Ministry staff are stirring them up, sowing discord where it does not really exist. Social action is unchristian. Any kind of farm labor organization is bad for the agricultural industry.

The local church withdrawal of financial support came as a discouraging blow, but it did not end the project. Support continued from the Northern and Southern California U.C.C. Conferences, the U.C.C. Board for Homeland Ministries and the Rosenberg Foundation. The Migrant Ministry also continued its support of the project, assuming responsibility for the salary and of Dave Havens. Hartmire's time was also allocated to assisting the project.

Drake was left unconvinced that the Migrant Ministry team could continue to work with the farm workers and still work for the church. In spite of the local congregation's actions, he was convinced that there were some magnificent people men in the church hierarchy who were behind the Migrant Ministry who would not leave them in the lurch. Especially notable, in Drake's recollection, was the support given them by the conference minister, Richard C. Norberg and his associate Walter S. Press. These two acted with great courage and conviction on the behalf of the T.C.C.D. team, and assured them that they were convinced of the validity of this ministry. These two ministers were subjected to great pressure, especially at local church and conference meetings, to take a more moderate stance, but they always held firmly to their convictions while demonstrating grace and compassion for others' positions.

Since Norberg and Press saw their role as interpretive and pastoral and since prominent leadership positions in many of their churches were filled by growers in the valley and in the bay area, these two spent countless hours in meetings, answering questions, explaining their viewpoints and allowing others to ventilate theirs. They also arranged for the growers' side of the issues to be heard publicly at conference and synod meetings. At the same time they strongly supported the beleaguered ministers in the rural towns. By their noble, faithful stance and their understanding responses, they held people together in a fellowship under great tension. It was this kind of steadfast ministry by many denominational executives which constituted one of the essential and little noticed elements in the success of the social change experienced here through church action.

The Migrant Ministry leadership saw clearly the meaning and effectiveness of these two rural fringe ministries. All of the rural fringe projects, despite the various types of communities and organizational styles, focused on the empowerment of farm workers. The commission's decision to commit the ministry to servanthood, to stand with the farm workers, assist their organizing efforts and to help them confront injustice in society, worked to some degree to redress the power imbalance. Achieving even small victories gave encouragement and strength to these new allies—church persons and farm workers. The alliance was growing.

7. Farm Worker-Minister Teams Develop

Meanwhile some organizational changes in the Migrant Ministry were taking place. In 1962 as commission chair I began working with Carl Seigenthaler and others to examine the Migrant Ministry's relationships with its constituent denominations and the amount of financial support given by each as well as the degree their executives were involved with this ministry. These studies led to major restructuring of the statewide ministries of the cooperating churches.

The California Church Council, first incorporated in 1916 but long dormant, was reactivated to serve as the vehicle for these ministries. Now with these structural modifications the Migrant Ministry had channels of authority and support which were clearer and more direct. When the need for action arose these lines of communication enabled rapid, strong response. These changes also enhanced and made more effective the statewide structure for ministry adopted during Dean Collins' incumbency. Basically they followed the direction given by the Division of Home Missions of the National Council of Churches, (N.C.C.), as steps to strengthen migrant ministries throughout the country.

Early in 1961 Douglas Still resigned as Migrant Ministry director to accept a position with the Chicago Council of Churches. In September of that year Chris Hartmire assumed the directorship. The transition was made easier because he was known to many in the Migrant Ministry, having been a summer program volunteer in his seminary years.

Among Hartmire's top priorities as he assumed his new duties were the community development training project, with

Ross and Chavez, in which he enrolled and the rural fringe ministries, especially in Tulare County. Both programs received Hartmire's close attention as he moved vigorously to help the state commission members understand the new servant ministry and its underlying theology of mission.

The commission membership included denominational executives and laity influential in their respective churches who welcomed this orientation. At each commission meeting there would be a session with educational content—a process which became an important factor in developing their mission strategy.

A major new ministry was created at this time to enable the church to serve the farm worker cause more effectively. Since a key concept of servanthood ministry involves standing with the poor in the sense of being with them in all aspects of their life and suffering, the Migrant Ministry sought to express this concept by establishing a farm worker-minister program. This brought together, in an organic relationship, two persons from different walks of life in a joint ministry of action.

Soon it became apparent that these newly formed farm worker-minister teams were a creative approach to social change which directly linked the church with the farm workers and their emerging union movement. The historical precedent for this worker-minister program came from the worker-priests in industrial France during the years after World War II. There priests had placed themselves at the "mercy" of the working classes, who by and large were outside the church. The Roman Catholic hierarchy had failed to give wholehearted support to this movement, so although some notable successes occurred it grew more slowly than anticipated and continues today as only a marginal movement.

The Migrant Ministry staff and the cooperating denominations came to this task having learned valuable lessons from their experimental community development work in the rural fringe ministries. From this solid base the farm worker-minister program grew. Several conclusions drawn from the direct involvement of farm workers in these projects became the conceptual basis for program relationships and were spelled out in a California Church

Council document which was published in 1965. In summary the paper said:

1). Seasonal farm workers can be organized for self-help action. What is needed are a catalyst, (staff person), some deeply-felt issues and a democratic structure.

2). Farm workers, acting together, can exert influence, challenge established injustices and improve conditions. When this happens, the whole community is served as formerly disenfranchised people join with dignity and strength to define the shape of community life.

3). Social change is accompanied by "people change." When leaders emerge and are trained, human needs are served and the sense of dignity of the participants is strengthened as they learn to use the tools of democracy in their own organization.

4). Staff people must expect to be tested by the community before trust can be established. There is already a deep, hostile chasm between the worker communities and the established communities in income, education and work experience which often set the staff person apart.

5). The emerging community group will tend to focus on neighborhood needs or labor issues, or both.

6). Supporting denominations in this program must be willing to let staff be responsive to the goals and tactics decided upon by the low income people.

These conclusions emerged from the proposal to establish the farm worker-minister program in California which had been presented by the Migrant Ministry to the California Church Council. Requirements for the proposed worker-ministers were that one of them would be a farm worker while the other would be a theologically sophisticated and articulate young clergy or lay person who was willing to live in a rural fringe area and who could demonstrate an ability for sustained work as a farm laborer.

It was further proposed that each worker-minister should earn from farm labor some $1,500 per year. The denominations involved agreed to pay each team member an additional $2,000 per year and also provide health insurance and participation in a pension plan. The denominational support made it possible for the team to engage in organizing yet it was not so large as to alienate the worker-ministers from their fellow workers or from each other. Thus each team included one middle class partner and one farm worker partner who together shared a common ministry. In most cases each made a two-year commitment to the community where they lived and worked.

The initial proposal sought to put four to six teams in the field during 1966 with the Migrant Ministry assuming responsibility for supervision and coordination as well as conducting the required intensive field training. The Migrant Ministry team also agreed to include in their role the structuring of careful, ongoing reflection and evaluation by the teams and supervisory staff.

The worker-minister program gave the church an opportunity to participate in a new form of servant ministry in its alliance with farm workers. The solidarity expressed through this relationship facilitated the bonding and further helped the allies to move forward in implementing their basic assumption that justice for farm workers required a new balance of power in the agricultural community.

A number of denominations provided funds and, in some cases, personnel thus becoming active participants in the program's progress. From its beginning in 1966 the program was an effective operation of the church and is still ongoing. In 1986 there were 15 individuals and their families involved in the ministry with an annual budget of $230,000. Through the years changes have been adopted in response to specific needs so that today they no longer work in teams but rather as individuals who work directly with the union.

During the 1960s while the Migrant Ministry was developing and implementing their various programs, other church groups and agencies also were involved in ministering to the needs of the migrant community. Many individuals sought to address the farm labor problem from different perspectives and with different strategies. Some examples of these actions were:

1). The Committee on Economic Justice in the Agricultural Community, (E.J.A.C.), appeared in early 1965 because its founders felt the Migrant Ministry was too narrow in its scope and criticised the Migrant Ministry's approach for only being related to farm workers. They expressed this concern by proposing a ministry designed to involve the total agricultural community including the growers, laborers, processors, shippers, wholesalers, retailers, consumers and government representatives. Their meetings included persons from all these categories.

In response the Migrant Ministry pointed out that the established church included and related well to persons from all these groups, except for farm workers. Therefore serving the workers in a democratic organization of their own choosing was a legitimate role for a separate ministry.

In reality, although the E.J.A.C. sought representation from all the listed categories, in actuality the growers and the church officials, including the State Councils of Churches, along with the industrial labor union officials predominated in the organization. In practice, the persons most directly affected, the farm workers, did not participate.

Chaired by Douglas Chalmers, president of a rubber firm and a Congregational church member, the E.J.A.C. sought to achieve reconciliation through discussions, seminars, study papers, fact-finding activities and consultations. Although many churches participated in E.J.A.C.'s program, what leaders did not take into account is that to achieve reconciliation the issue of power must be addressed. Their process did not do that nor did the E.J.A.C. leaders contemplate specific action programs for themselves—although they did make recommendations for action to the California Church Council.

E.J.A.C. functioned until October 1971. It could be credited as having been moderately effective in providing an increased awareness of the farm worker situation. The California Church Council viewed it as primarily an advisory body. Their funding never reached the hoped for level and without staff the E.J.A.C. was unable to make a significant impact. One reason for this may well be that the persons involved lacked any real desire to change their own ways or their relationships. Like the Conference on Families Who Follow the Crops (see below) E.J.A.C. identified problems, displayed differing perspectives and needs, but none of the participating entities were willing to give up power or to alter the status quo in any way.

The Migrant Ministry staff and commission viewed with suspicion those involved with promoting E.J.A.C., interpeting their motives to be development of E.J.A.C. as a potential vehicle to neutralize C.M.M. effectiveness. Their "study and educate" approach, often used in many contexts in the church, is considered by many to be an effective way of postponing (i.e. denying) any meaningful actions which might be conducive to real social change.

2). The Conference on Families Who Move with the Crops was another effort to try to bring opposing sides to a reasoned discussion. Douglas Still, along with Mrs. Florence Wycoff, a member of the California Governor's Advisory Committee on Child Abuse, and Bard McAllister, a staff person with the American Friends Service Committee who was much opposed to the church using Alinsky methods, joined forces to organize a rather extensive series of conferences to consider migrant worker needs. They sponsored these meetings in cooperation with state agencies and the California Farm Bureau Federation and were quite successful in involving most all the pertinent establishment segments of society. Although they claimed to have farm workers included in their conferences, those workers who were actually selected as delegates all came from middle class organizations.

For nearly three years these organizers made a good faith effort with this process, but had little to show for their labors. The participants reached almost universal consensus on the problems of farm workers, but almost no agreement was reached on solutions. Neither growers nor government officials showed any willingness to give any power to or to deal with a farm worker organization directly. In the words of Douglas Still, who had high hopes when they organized the conferences, "I would say it was a total failure, absolutely, completely a bust!"

3). The Special Committee of Nine was appointed by the Presbytery of San Joaquin, Presbyterian Church USA, to recommend a policy guide for a responsible and prudent Christian response to the Delano strike. Its report was adopted April 18,

1966, by the presbytery. In essence the committee commended
the Migrant Ministry for its "empathy for and identification with
the farm worker," but cautioned it not to identify with one group
so as to become the opponent of other groups.

It further proposed that the California Church Council undertake, among other steps, the formation of the "California Ministry
to the Agricultural Community" (C.M.A.C.) and requested that
the worker-minister program *not be* implemented within the
bounds of the presbytery until an alternate program had been
worked out. This action effectively blocked $4,000 in funds al-
ready approved by the Presbyterian Board of National Missions
for a worker-minister program in the Presbytery. Neither the
C.M.A.C. nor an alternative program were ever developed.

4). The California Ministry to the Agricultural Community
(C.M.A.C.), which had been proposed by the Committee of Nine,
was presented to the California Church Council at a meeting of
the E.J.A.C.)Committee, not at a regular meeting of the council.
Its stated purpose was to act as a ministry of dialogue between
the growers and the workers, between the Migrant Ministry and
the growers and between clergy and the growers, farm workers
and the Migrant Ministry. They posited that if communications
could be kept open reconciliation would be possible. The program
was not implemented.

5). Christian Action With Farm Workers was a proposal
which never went beyond the draft stage. Envisioned, essentially,
as a plan for continuing the alliance between Christian individuals
and farm workers as they formed their own union, it was seen
as independent of denominational and interdenominational supervision. At the planning level it was intended to maintain a close
relationship with the Migrant Ministry, but was really a fallback
plan, devised by Hartmire and Drake, to be available in case the
Tulare County Community Development Project was completely
terminated in Porterville. Although it was never needed, that it
existed at the planning level is proof of the determination of these
two people to be faithful to their commitments with farm workers.

Even though these alternative approaches to ministry to farm
workers were well-intentioned in themselves, none, with the

exception of the last, recognized the fundamental problem of the powerlessness of farm workers. The great majority of church members had no preparation to deal with the controversial dynamics of the use of power in society. These alternative plans forcused on reconciliation through dialogue, and study, good will through increased understanding of the conditions of work in the fields, ignoring in their conceptualization the dimensions of the power relationships of labor and management in agribusiness.

To fully understand the Migrant Minstry's theology of mission, it is crucial for one to perceive clearly the dynamics of economic power. With such an understanding of the forces at work in society, one's ability to serve oppressed peoples is enhanced. With such increased insight one can serve them in ways that are effective, yet at the same time be careful to affirm their self-worth and dignity, helping to release the latent power of the poor to solve their own problems. Through this understanding the church can become a partner and servant rather than a parent or supervisor.

8. Pictorial Reflections

A transportable communion table is set up for the farm workers.

The Harvester brings good news to farm worker children.

On site child care was an early emphasis of the migrant ministry.

Typical farm worker housing.

Cesar Chavez leads a home meeting discussion.

Dolorez Huerta, vice-president and chief negotiator for the United Farm Workers Union, leads a meeting in the California Union Hall, Salinas, 1970.

Chris Hartmire at the podium of a strike meeting in Negrito Hall, Delano, 1966.

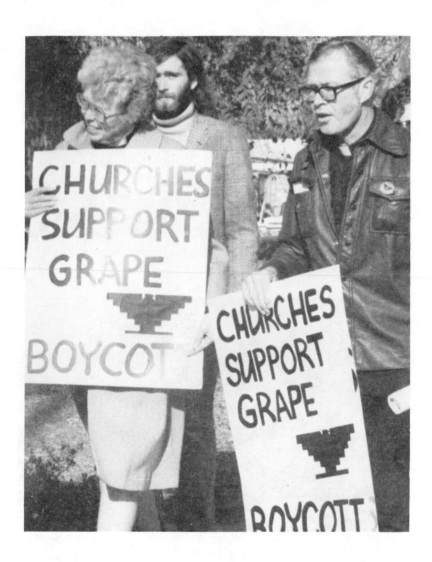

Clergy join the march protesting farm worker conditions.

The pilgrimage wends its way to Sacramento.

The Philippine farm workers join the strike.

Clergy join the march protesting farm worker conditions.

Bobby Kennedy and other farm worker supporters gather to break
bread with Cesar Chavez at the conclusion of his 25 day fast for
nonviolence.

9. The Farm Worker Union Is Born

After World War II, many Mexican-American citizens, mostly young, refused to accept discrimination as a new feeling of selfhood and dignity stirred among them. A middle class developed in this group as they prospered. This occurred more readily in urban centers than in rural areas. With ethnic awareness, seeing themselves as Chicanos, they demanded better treatment by society. Returned veterans often got better education, housing and jobs under the G.I. Bill of Rights and in this way some achieved modest economic and political power.

Still most Chicanos lived in abject poverty and felt, psychologically if not physically, confined to their barrios and colonias. Police brutality constantly reminded them of their inferior status in the eyes of the dominant white community. Barriers remained in jobs, housing, politics and social life.

Although these postwar changes expanded the Chicanos personal sense of worth, bringing them to a new level of self-esteem, change came slowly and with great effort. Most of their real gains came through self-help efforts. The Community Services Organization, (C.S.O.), was a major result of this awakening. Here poor people, striving for justice in their lives, began using this democratic, social change organization to work in their own behalf.

Pedro Garcia, an early leader in the C.S.O., once described the context from which it emerged to me, "Before the C.S.O., whenever one of us Mexicans had a problem, regardless of whether the problem was with the police department, our streets, our lights, some health problem, the schools or what have you, we were always sent to the dog catcher. That job was always filled, by either political party with a Spanish speaking person who not only served as the link between the authorities and the Spanish speaking population—but actually was the authority!"

He went on to explain what this meant to the Hispanic community, "This was very bad for all our people. Imagine, everytime something came up regarding the city we would all have to go to the dog catcher! But not anymore! Not since the C.S.O.!"

The Community Services Organization had sprung up in Los Angeles in 1946 and was seen by a small group of World War II veterans as a vehicle for addressing their problems. Later one of these veterans, Edward Roybal, was elected to the Los Angeles City Council and then went on to congress representing California's 25th District.

The great bulk of C.S.O. membership consisted of low-income Mexican Americans so the extensive programs they developed focused on their immediate needs—including English instruction, citizenship education and voter registration. Soon the C.S.O. had become an effective vehicle for achieving significant social change for its members.

Two key figures in the C.S.O., subsequently involved in the creation of the future union of farm workers, were Cesar Chavez—a migrant farm worker himself—and Fred Ross. The C.S.O. had turned to Saul Alinsky, founder of the Industrial Areas Foundation (I.A.F.), to help in its own organizing activity.

In 1947 Alinsky, impressed by his experience and sensitive organizing skills, hired Ross, who in turn, in 1953 hired and trained Chavez in San Jose, California. Chavez, a very apt pupil, became an outstanding organizer for the C.S.O., and eventually was appointed its national training director in 1958. This training was to be invaluable experience to Chavez in terms of his future goals.

The C.S.O. achieved an exceptionally successful record in voter registration—which was to be its base for the development of its power for social change. The September 26, 1960 National C.S.O. report of California activity listed 500 deputy registrars who were going door-to-door. With 120,000 hours of effort they had signed up 137,096 new registrants throughout the state.

In Fresno that year a joint registration effort of the League of Women Voters, the American Legion, the P.T.A. and the A.F.L./C.I.O. between January and April registered only 205 persons. In a third of that time the C.S.O. registered 2,704 people.

The importance of skilled staff was stressed in the Industrial Areas Foundation Annual Report for 1958-59. As a way of example they pointed out what a good organizer could do. They noted that Chavez, who had been sent to Oxnard on his first assignment, was able to log the following achievements for a nascent union within eleven months: 1). Semi-monthly meetings were being held with an average attendance of 450, 2). The recruiting of 950 members who were paying monthly dues of four dollars each, 3). The enrolling 650 people in semiweekly citizenship classes, 4). Organizing a credit union, 5). Operating a continuous rummage sale which was clearing $200 per month, 6). The maintenance of a service center—open 18 hours daily, seven days per week with 30 volunteers, 7). Registering 300 new voters, putting on the most intensive get- out-the-vote campaign in C.S.O. history, 8). Conducting an organizing program among field workers which resulted in the replacement by local workers of hundreds of Mexican nationals—"braceros" (This was the first time field workers had ever been organized) and 9). Getting the state to investigate grower hiring practices. (The investigation proved that there had been collusion between growers and State Farm Placement Service officers in discriminatory employment.)

Commenting later on the Oxnard results, Fred Ross said, "Forcing the growers to hire local workers instead of braceros was a significant development. But of deeper significance was the fact that Chavez now knew that a union of field workers could be organized and that he could do it!"

With this success behind him Chavez felt confident enough to resign his job with the C.S.O. in order to be free to build a union. Other factors also influenced Chavez' decision. By 1962 its membership also included some middle-income persons. Often they shared interests and concerns with the original low-income founders, but their priorities were decidely different. Strains began to appear. Mixing the poor with the middle-class persons made for an inherently unstable situation which eventually changed the direction of the organization, moving it into a less radical, more socially acceptable, operating mode.

In Alinsky's view, to improve its lot, a group of poor folk must use confrontational tactics to address specific problems, since such methods could lead dramatically to successful, if disruptive, change. Gradually, the middle class members of the group tended to pull away since it was in their best interest to favor compromise and accommodation and avoid confrontation. The poorest members of the community, however, needed the organization and its direct action to accomplish their goals.

Essentially because of this shift of priorities away from direct action on behalf of the low-income members, Chavez failed to get C.S.0. backing for the unionizing of field workers. On March 31, 1962—his 35th birthday—he resigned his position and along with his wife, Helen; and their eight children, moved back to Delano, California where Cesar and Helen had met years before when he was a field hand himself.

The long struggle to build a union of, by and for farm workers now began. For years Chavez had studied the many strikes in California and had even kept extensive notes on them, analyzing their sucesses and failures and identifying strategies which worked. This intensive study served him well, now, as he faced the challenge of creating a union.

Many before him had tried in the 20th century to organize a union among the field workers in California. The list is prestigious—the Industrial Workers of the World (Wobblies); the United Cannery Workers; the Agricultural, Packing and Allied Workers of America; The United Packinghouse Workers of America; the Food, Tobacco and Agricultural Workers Union; the A.F.L.; the C.I.O.; and the Teamsters.

All these unions had faced a formidable task. For over a century California growers had employed countless foreign and domestic workers. During this period many contractual and informal arrangements had evolved which were substitutes for just labor relations. Growers offered extremely low wages under harsh working conditions. No union was going to upset their power if they had anything to say about it.

Even though the severe working conditions, coupled with employer discrimination, had already produced hundreds of strikes, since the growers had the power, the land, the crops and the money, there was little improvement. In some cases wages and conditions improved temporarily, but never were contracts signed or any lasting gains achieved by the workers. Also since these strikes had occurred in scattered areas and were usually led by persons from outside the barrio, the indigenous leadership was ignored and failure was foreordained.

Having studied the history of farm worker strikes and feeling ebullient and strengthened by his success in the C.S.O., Chavez vowed to avoid some of the fatal mistakes of his predecessors. By using the techniques which he and Ross had learned while in the C.S.O., Chavez began organizing hundreds of house meetings—a Ross device—where he encouraged the farm workers to talk about their many problems. During these discussions he would suggest the possibility of working together to form an association in which they could resolve some of their mutual concerns. Carefully, he avoided alarming those who might fear a union because of previous bad experiences with organizers.

All along Chavez was determined to organize slowly, one member at a time, without holding out false hopes of contracts or recognition. These results would come later when the association had enough strength to withstand the inevitable sacrifices it must make. With few illusions, even in the early days, Chavez foresaw that this would be a long struggle which might take at least five years. Having learned that most agricultural strikes were decided in the first few weeks he resolved, "No strikes until we get organized!"

He vowed that, most importantly, his farm worker's union would be a union of and by the poor. The success Chavez achieved in accomplishing this goal came through his wise and skillful choice of associates. That spring of 1962, in order to build a militant and democratic union of farm workers paid for by farm workers and run by farm workers, Chavez traveled to every farming community in the San Joaquin Valley seeking out those farm workers who understood the need for organization and who would be willing to pay $3.50 per month in dues. Chavez refused to offer little in immediate expectations of benefit, promising nothing but hard work and real risk. The dues charged were to be the test of intention. Those who stopped paying were dropped without any cajoling. Chavez himself received no salary. Helen, and Cesar too when he had time, worked in the fields to provide the family with a meager living.

On September 30, 1962, Chavez called together a few hundred workers—men, women and children—to the founding convention of the National Farm Workers Association, (N.F.W.A.). Even in choosing a name Chavez avoided the term, union.

This rather unprepossing group met in a dusty, abandoned theater in Fresno, California. Cesar and Helen Chavez were joined by other organizers: Dolores Huerta, Antonio Orendain and later Gil Padilla of the California Center for Community Development team and Larry Itliong of the Agriculture Workers Organizing Committee. In this rickety surroundings, with a great and historic leap of faith, this group of determined, committed farm workers founded the N.F.W.A.. Hartmire and Drake, of the Migrant Ministry, also were present.

No newsperson, historian, grower or politician foresaw the full consequences of this event nor suspected that this group of the poorest of the poor, in this bold and courageous act, were creating a nationwide movement which would bring about fundamental change in agricultural labor relations in California and, eventually, the nation.

The organizers, however, knew what they were up against. As Chavez has sinced explained, "The power of the growers was backed by the political power of the police, the courts, the state and the federal laws and by the financial power of the big corporations, the banks and utilities."

It took the singleminded zeal that Chavez and his associates were demonstrating to begin sucessfully to organize California field workers. (They had been unionized in Hawaii several years earlier). With their union, farm workers for the first time began to gain public recognition as well as an increasing feeling of worth.

At this time the workers began to set their own goals. Foremost in their minds was to achieve public acceptance on the part of the growers that farm workers had a right to organize their own union on the basis of human dignity and justice. It was also decided that they would not accept employers into the union. The aim of this effort was, of course, to get a labor contract which would stipulate the desparately needed improvements in wages and working conditions.

As incentives to keep the members in the union, Chavez provided benefits to N.F.W.A. members which included a co-op store, a gas station and a service center in Porterville. Paid up members were also given a very modest life insurance policy—all as part of their $3.50 per month dues. Chavez personally was available to help association members in any family or personal crises.

Chavez later explained the two guiding principles of those days: First, since there was no money in the coffers and the job had to be done, there would have to be a lot of sacrificing on everyone's part. Second, no matter how poor the people in the association were, they had a responsibility to help the union. If they had two dollars for food, they had to give one dollar to the union. Otherwise they would never get out of the trap of poverty. They would never have a union because they couldn't afford to sacrifice a little bit more on top of their everyday misery.

Because he was willinig to live sacrificially Chavez was able to call on all farm workers in the association to join him in these sacrifices. The following three years were filled with painstaking, thorough, hard, and at times, discouraging efforts to build the union based on justice for farm workers. By mid-1965, however, the union had a loyal membership of 1,200—even though only some 200 were able to pay dues regularly out of their meager incomes.

10. *La Huelga*

Suddenly a crucial event occurred which precipitated events. Another union, the Agricultural Workers Organizing Committee (A.W.O.C.) called for a strike at the very center of the table grape industry—in Delano, located in the southern San Joaquin valley of California. Founded in 1959 by the AFL-CIO, A.W.O.C. later was to go out of existence, in 1966, when the N.F.W.A. merged with A.W.O.C. to form the United Farm Workers Organizing Committee (U.F.W.O.C.) with Cesar Chavez, of the N.F.W.A., director and Larry Itliong, of the A.W.O.C., as the associate director.

The strike began on September 8, 1965 when A.W.O.C. convinced a large group of farm workers to walk out of the vineyards. Between 600 and 800 workers, mostly Filipino, joined in the strike demanding the right to bargain with their employers for fair wages and just working conditions. Many of the strikers were longtime residents of Delano who each year traveled first to the Coachela Valley, in the southeast corner of the state, where the grape harvest occurs earlier than in Delano. That year, in Coachella, they were paid $1.40 per hour, plus an incentive piece rate. Returning to Delano the workers were distressed to learn that the growers were unwilling to pay such a wage. Instead, they were offering to pay $1.25 hourly, with a lower piece rate.

The union sent letters to the large employers asking for a meeting to discuss wages and working conditions and to negotiate a contract. These letters went unanswered. The workers then publicly announced they would call a strike if the employers refused to enter into good faith bargaining. Again there was no response from the employers. When the growers disdainfully ignored their public call for negotiations the workers had no choice but to strike, or lose face. *La Huelga* was on!

Soon the Filipino workers of the A.W.O.C. asked Chavez and the N.F.W.A. to join their strike. Although Cesar felt the union was not yet strong enough to maintain a successful strike he believed in the right of the members, acting democratically, to speak on their own behalf. He put it to a vote.

They voted YES. Quickly, they decided to join their brothers and sisters. Chavez accepted this mandate but then asked for another vote. This time the question was to commit themselves to maintain nonviolent tactics in the strike. Again they voted in the affirmative. To Chavez this vote was of utmost importance for it established the principle of nonviolence from the outset—it assured the integrity of the movement and affirmed this quality of his leadership.

As these dramatic events unfolded, the church through its agency, the Migrant Ministry, made a clear-cut decision to stand with the union. Moreover, the Migrant Ministry staff and commission—clergy and laity—decided to join actively in well-publicized confrontations by workers in their bold challenge to the overwhelmingly powerful growers. It was these actions which cemented the alliance of the church with the workers. Since the strike and subsequent events have been fully documented in detail in Jacques Levy's *Cesar Chavez—Autobiography of La Causa* and in other accounts, our discussion will be confined to the faith community/farm worker relationship as it was strengthened during the strike.

It was on the picket lines that Migrant Ministry volunteers came into contact with local police and sheriff's deputies—as well as with strikebreakers (often illegal immigrants brought in for this specific purpose) and grower personnel.

Soon headlines around the country screamed the story and pictures of clergy, adorned with clerical collars, covered the front pages. When Hartmire and others were arrested, the Migrant Ministry's stand was unmistakably clear to everyone throughout the whole land.

One valley pastor, Bill Dew, remembers being confronted

by church members who were also growers: Rather than argue with the parishioners regarding how much the workers should be paid, which he felt was not his issue, he instead discussed his own views of the nature and purpose of the church and its ministry. When someone raised the question of a clergy person being on the strike line, he found it appropriate to move the discussion to their understanding of the role of an ordained person. In his experience he found the laity responded very positively to such a dialogue.

The Migrant Ministry at the time was able to set up many support groups which functioned well. A trickle and then a flood of people joined these groups. Supporters came from several Jewish bodies, the major Protestant mainline denominations, the Catholic church, the National Council of Churches and the World Council of Churches. Also students and other young people from around the country, members of local churches, labor unions and labor federations in the U.S., Canada and even several foreign countries joined the farm worker movement. Much of this volunteer advocacy was coordinated by Chris Hartmire who along with Chavez spoke widely on campuses, at rallys, in churches and at judicatory meetings raising support. Persons from all walks of life caught the vision and became evangelists for *La Causa*.

There were, however, critics among the church members and some clergy who condemned the Migrant Ministry for siding with the union. This alliance, they said, was partisan and political when instead the church should be seeking reconciliation through negotiation or mediation. Some described the alliance as unchristian and failed to acknowledge that even in a strike, acting nonviolently, alone, can be a reconciling activity. They could not accept the concept that powerless, oppressed persons must gain and use some power by withholding their labor before their powerful adversaries would negotiate with them.

For years farm workers had lived and worked under violent, oppressive conditions which are well documented in numerous private and public studies of the conditions of migrant labor. These studies of the substandard nature of their employment invariably showed increased incidence of disease, higher accident rates and lessened life expectancy among farm workers. Further, workers were degraded by these conditions and suffered psychic and physical harm.

Growers tended to treat their workers paternalistically and, by their attitudes, essentially denied workers any human worth. Racism and class bias underlay grower relationships with the very people on whom their enterprise depended. By conducting a strike nonviolently workers not only affirmed the validity and worth of growers, but displayed—in stark contrast to grower attitudes—a more humane and positive attitude.

Throughout, the Migrant Ministry staff acted on their belief that workers, as mature humans, possessed the right to good faith bargaining. When the workers chose to use nonviolence, they not only demonstrated their belief in the dignity of their adversary, but likewise they were demanding they be accepted as equals. This attitude left the door open to reconciliation because they clearly were proposing negotiation rather than attempting to destroy the system or a particular grower's business. This was understood by many in the church to be a profoundly Christian position.

Two specific events occurred which led up to the strike and which emboldened the strikers to defy their employers and take strike action while at the same time it united and strengthened the resolve of the farm workers and their church allies. Both are worthy of note.

The first incident took place during the spring of 1965 when the N.F.W.A. was asked to back the wage demands of the workers at the Mt. Arbor Rose Nursery in McFarland. At that time the Migrant Ministry and the Tulare County Community Development Project (T.C.C.D.) were asked to provide staff assistance. Since it was determined that the request was consistent with the staff assignment—"to help farm workers organize for self-help action of a kind that they define, targeted on goals they determine"—they decided to comply. To avoid undue controversy over his participation, however, Jim Drake decided to take a "vacation" from his position so his assistance would be unofficial until the decision could be cleared with key U.C.C. people and the Migrant Ministry Commission.

The second event where Migrant Ministry staff support was requested by the farm workers involved a rent strike at some farm labor camps run by the Tulare County Housing Authority. Here families lived at Linnel and Woodville in 30-year old ramshackle buildings which had been allowed to deteriorate, receiving but minimal maintenance over the years. When the authorities announced a major rent increase, effective immediately, the workers refused to pay. The Migrant Ministry staff endorsed the workers response and were pleased when the state stepped in and ruled that there would be no rent increases.

Although neither of these actions achieved much success in terms of union goals, still the Mt. Arbor Nursery did increase their pay rates modestly and the Housing Authority improved some of the rules governing conditions at Linnel and Woodville. The most significant result of these two events, in which the farm workers' organization and the Migrant Ministry jointly participated, was the progressively close relationship which developed out of the joint experience.

Since events not only educate but also determine future action, Hartmire subsequently issued, in July of 1967 a case study reflecting on the significance of these events. Called *The Church and the Emerging Farm Worker Movement*, it discusses what Hartmire saw as nine important Migrant Ministry policies which were set following these actions. Hartmire's thesis is that these insights, learned in the process of joint action, prepared the California Migrant Ministry (C.M.M.) and denominational executives for the hard decisions they would later make to support farm workers and their democratic union. His nine points are:

1). A shift in C.M.M. programing from a service only operation (services instead of justice) to the support of self-help action (assuming a servanthood role).

2). A close working relationship between Chavez' N.F.W.A. and the C.M.M.

3). The staff involvement in useful conflict in the church and the community as in the bracero struggle and the rural fringe ministries.

4). The denominational staff's experience in these controversies.

5). Developing trustworthy working relationships between the C.M.M. staff and the denominational staffs, primarily in the rural fringe ministries.

6). The loss, during the bracero struggle, of financial support from those opposed to social change which prepared the church for future financial loss during the strike controversy and taught the Migrant Ministry to live with leaner, better-focused budgets.

7). The shift of the oversight of the C.M.M. from the National Council of Churches to the California Church Council on January 1, 1965. This drew the California denominations closer together in support of the strike, and also helped cut the C.M.M. program budget to a manageable size which, of necessity, focused on the highest priority programs.

8). The policy deliberations which took place over the rose nursery strike prepared the staff to act decisively later in the Delano grape strike.

9). The decision to stay out of direct sponsorship of programs funded by the federal Office of Economic Opportunity, (O.E.O.). Hartmire deemed as "hypocritical nonsense" acceptance of such funding, since to talk about fighting poverty among farm workers made no sense if you refused to support their drive for union organization and collective bargaining.

These progressively crucial decisions were significant as the C.M.M. staff, commission and denominations were led ever closer to full support of this particular association of farm workers and the N.F.W.A. Hartmire concluded this reflection by saying, "It is also important to note that without this pioneering penetration, the churches would not have been in a position to understand the strikers or support them in their time of need: nor would we have been able to bring our influence and our hopefulness about life to bear in a tense and, at times, hopeless situation. Gospel communication and influence are tied inextricably to servanthood. There seems no other way!"

Support for the striking farm workers eventually came from many sources. Important backing came through the universities and colleges. Some 20 college students, volunteers in the 1965 C.M.M. summer program, were assigned to work directly with farm workers, participating in their daily lives. In the fall when they returned to school they had developed new insights into the problems of migrant workers. Their middle class perceptions had been profoundly altered by sharing in the distress of the truly poor. Eventually, when middle class Americans were touched by this college-age enthusiasm, understanding and support rapidly spread through direct communication to churches, unions and other voluntary groups.

When the farm workers decided to go on strike in September, many of these students not only were the union's most enthusiastic supporters, but also they were anxious to help organize and stimulate other students to boycott, picket, leaflet and raise funds on behalf of the strikers. During this period Chavez visited many campus holding rallies among students, effectively recruiting many volunteers and supporters from among students and faculty. From the ferment created by these actions at colleges and universities the union gained faithful and dedicated supporters.

The Delano grape strike, which was to go on for five long years, pitted a relatively small, but powerful, group of some 32 growers who adamantly refused to recognize the N.F.W.A. in any way against a union which was gradually gaining enough power to bring increasing economic pressure on these growers. With dogged persistance the union pursued its goals under the profound spiritual motivation of Chavez' leadership which gave his *huelgistas* the backbone to persevere. It was this spiritual leadership, more than any other factor, which allowed this strike eventually to succeed where others, throughout history, had failed.

Never can the National Farm Workers Association, later called the United Farm Workers Union—AFL/CIO (U.F.W.), under Chavez be seen as a typical labor union. Tactics heretofore unknown to labor were used to good effect, including diverse and creative methods to generate support combined with a unique sensitivity to ethnic strengths and customs which came out of Chavez' personal ethic, his deep Christian faith and moral character, and his commitment to nonviolence. Subsistence level salaries for union staff and members, and later the Migrant Ministry staff, meant that everyone who committed themselves to this labor movement shared the life-style of the very poor. Truly an exceptional achievement.

These unique features of the N.F.W.A. contributed to the union's ultimate success. Three resultant factors can be cited: 1). The widespread support by the middle class; 2). The solidarity which developed between the farm workers union, the AFL/CIO and many international trade unions; and 3). The alliance of the union with the religious community through the Migrant Ministry.

These factors resulted, in part, from Chavez use of politically potent tactics:

1). The Boycott against grape growers and eventually against a giant supermarket conglomerate—Safeway Stores, Inc.;

2). *La Peregrinacion* (The Pilgrimage), most notably, the long and well publicized march from Delano to Sacramento, capital of California, in 1966, along with other effective uses of the tactic of a march on other occasions;

3). The Fast, which was undertaken on several occasions by Chavez and others.

Although these fasts were often misunderstood and denigrated by the critics, they played a major part in maintaining morale among the striking workers. When the abuse and violence suffered at the hands of strikebreakers sorely tried the farm workers resolve to be nonviolent, the powerful spiritual force developed through these fasts somehow seemed to make the difference and kept them from responding violently.

The Boycott

Without question it was the boycott which was the most effective and widely used tactic developed by Chavez and his *huelgistas*. This time-honored nonviolent social change device was used as a skillful weapon to reach the vast middle class of America. With Chavez' insights into human nature, he creatively captured public opinion for *La Causa*, and soon the press was widely reporting boycott activity. The resulting publicity reached a broad spectrum of the middle class which could easily understand the issues thus presented and were led to respond appropriately.

This widespread publicity also gave Chavez the opportunity to emphasize nonviolence as the union's guiding principle. This was a great recruiting incentive and motivated many to participate in the movement. In various speeches Chavez often said, "The growers have the money and clout but we have our time and our bodies. We will win."

The Delano grape boycott had far-reaching consequences for it focused nationwide attention on the farm worker movement. Churches all over the country began to respond because church people could comprehend the necessity for a boycott, seeing it as a tactic which was consistent with their ethical teaching and was a legitimate way to effect peaceful social change.

To capitalize on this growing national support Chavez sent farm workers to the major cities of this country and Canada to urge people to support the grape boycott. This was an incredibly difficult mission for these unsophisticated farm workers who for the most part had never been to the East coast. Many knew little English and found it difficult to make their way around. Although they were scared and timid, their audacious determination, coupled with the spiritual power of the movement, impelled them to work to the outer limits of their strength and faith. On their return home these simple folk told countless stories of their growth-producing experiences through which they gained self-esteem and confidence.

More importantly, they spread the boycott to many cities through their selfless efforts. Typically, they would approach churches, unions or other prospective friends in a poignant and personal manner. "I've come to Boston to stop the sale of grapes. I have only $1.56 so I need a place to work and live. Will you please help?"

The persuasiveness of such an approach, coupled with the sincerity of their testimonies about their working conditions, was irresistable to many people in the churches who responded with strong advocacy, working to commit their communities, churches and judicatories to the cause. Soon these people were saying, "We must help. They need money. Let's publicize the boycott. Get volunteers. Check it out with the C.M.M."

With such rapid and effective grass roots response and communication, it is no wonder the movement grew and the churches' alliance grew with it.

In retrospect, the development of the boycott can be viewed in the perspective of four separate phases:

At first the boycott actions were directed primarily against the DiGiorgio Farms and the Schenley Industries. Both of these firms were wine grape growers with well-known products— S. & W. Fine Foods and the Treesweet juices among them. This made it easier to ask consumers to stop buying these brand name products. Soon other activities emerged to further the boycott: leafleting, press conferences, visits by Chavez and others in the movement to colleges, churches and union halls.

Schenley was the first winery to agree to a contract, soon followed by several smaller wineries run by some Catholic orders. It has been speculated that Schenley may have been the first to agree to a contract because the company, through its distillery business, was accustomed to dealing with organized labor. The Delano growers had no such experience with unions and were much harder to convince.

A second phase which began in the spring of 1967 focused on the Giumarra Vineyards, the largest Delano table grape grower. Soon, the nationwide call went out, "Don't buy Giumarra grapes." Because grapes are delivered to stores in clearly labeled boxes, again it was not difficult for consumers to identify Giumarra grapes thus permitting an accurate, specific targeting of the boycott. This tactic was designed to increase the pressure on Giumarra products, especially after some smaller growers signed contracts, because then the public could be urged to buy "good" grapes rather than the "bad" Giumarra grapes.

By the late summer of 1967 Guimarra was hurt by the boycott, but instead of signing a contract they decided to retaliate and convinced other Delano growers to allow them to use their labels on Giumarra grape boxes. Since this made it impossible for consumers to identify the Guimarra grapes in the market, a new strategy on the part of the union was required to offset Guimarra's somewhat deceitful tactic.

The deceptive labeling led to a third phase in the boycott, begun in January of 1968, when the union expanded its boycott to include all table grapes. The call which now went out—"Don't buy table grapes!"—began to appear everywhere from billboards and bulletins to bumper stickers.

To add pressure to this effort a fourth phase of the boycott began in October 1968 when the focus shifted from the products themselves to their outlets. Soon, the chain stores which handled table grapes were faced with mounting pressure as farm worker union members and their supporters began passing out leaflets at stores, holding press conferences, and speaking in churches and communities. In the Eastern states several campaigns were conducted targeting their efforts on the major grocery chains such as the A & P stores. In 1970 Safeway became the major target in the lettuce boycott.

Some critics who opposed the goals of the farm workers began attacking the union for its boycotting of the supermarkets, charging the union with conducting a secondary boycott, illegal conduct under the National Labor Relations Act. However, since agricultural labor had been specifically exempted from that act when it was enacted in the 1930s, these charges did not legally apply to a farm worker union. The union thus was legitimately able to orchestrate its carefully conceived boycott of table grapes by focusing nationwide activity on the market chains. This later was extended even to some locations in European countries as well as in Hong Kong, Taiwan and Japan.

Primarily the boycott was carried out by picketing large stores and passing out informative leaflets in supermarket parking lots, a tactic which brought the farm worker struggle directly to the urban consumers in a most visible way. The Migrant Ministry staff, commission members and related organizations such as the Church Women United, worked tirelessly and effectively getting out the word.

Boycott committees, set up by the U.F.W. around the country and staffed by union members and volunteers including many young people from colleges, carried on the boycott. Local groups of church members formed support committees who donated food and money and, at the same time, joined the boycott activity in their city. Soon this very effective network functioned nationwide, attracting volunteers from middle class America, which was now aroused by the strike. These volunteers had accepted the call to action for a cause they could believe in. As volunteers, young and old, joined in solidarity with farm workers, a large network of church supporters of the Migrant Ministry came into being. Interfaith committees to aid farm workers appeared across the land.

The recruitment process generally was low-key. A *Sopa* often was held in a local church where a simple meal of soup and bread was served. Union songs would be sung by the group in Spanish and English, usually led by a young guitarist, setting the spirit of the meeting. As participants gave reports of boycotting activity, some of the farm workers testified with stories of their own struggles for dignity and a decent wage. One attending such a meeting came away with a strong feeling of solidarity with the the union and a desire to help.

Since personal testimonies were not polished speeches but, rather, heartfelt expressions of the reality of farm worker life, they were extremely effective. Soon strong bonds were forged between middle class folk and the farm workers through these experiences. Chavez and other union or Migrant Ministry leaders often spoke at these *Sopa* gatherings to give encouragement to this solidarity and to reinforce the union's commitment to nonviolence. The violence committed by the growers' foremen, sherriff deputies and strikebreakers was difficult for the workers to face alone. Having these church supporters experience the violence, both vicariously in these meeting and alongside farm workers on the boycott, built strong morale in the group.

As the boycott grew and spread throughout the country its impact and its effectiveness became apparent. The volunteers, both from the churches and the union, learned what true commitment cost. The union's public acts—reasonable, nonviolent, and easy to understand—reached a great many middle class consumers.

The boycott grew to tremendous proportions. As consumers refrained from buying grapes, growers began to be hurt. This nationwide, popularly supported boycott was the major factor in achieving an acceptance of the union which led to collective bargaining and the ultimate signing of contracts. Growers, although reluctantly, felt they had no other choice. No one ever accused them of entering this new relationship with joy.

La Peregrinacion

A more unusual tactic used by Chavez was *La Peregrinacion* (The Pilgrimage). The pilgrimage is culturally a common Mexican event, essentially Catholic in nature, but as used by Chavez it took on political overtones. The most widely publicized of the pilgrimages attracted attention all the way from Delano to the steps of the State Capitol Building in Sacramento, where it ended with a giant rally, attended by over 10,000 people, on Easter Sunday, 1966.

La Peregrinacion was decided on in response to a heinous act on the part of the Schenley Company management which had allowed some union pickets to be sprayed from the air, "accidently," with poisonous pesticide. This dramatic and forceful response was chosen because of its potential impact on the public conscience, but also to reinforce Chavez' call to the workers to renew their vows of nonviolence in the face of such persecution.

Once Chavez described *La Peregrinacion*, begun in Delano on March 16, 1966 in the following words, "At the front we had the American Flag, the Mexican flag, the flag from the Philippines and the banner of Our Lady of Guadalupe. People wore hats bearing the union's red hatbands with the black eagle, and many of the strikers wore red armbands with the black eagle and carried the *huelga* flags. Out in the country it was a thin, serpentine line inching its way along the flat valley with lots of red flags silhouetted against the blue sky. The first day there were more than a hundred marching as some of the wives and kids had come. There were about 70 who planned to walk all the way."

The march became a media event which created an awareness in a broader spectrum of society. The colorful column of campesinos, trudging along the highway, grew rapidly in importance. At first A.W.O.C.'s Al Green opposed the march and tried to keep the Philippino members out. They couldn't resist joining this event, which had emerged from a common religious and cultural heritage which they shared with the Mexicans. Strong words passed between Green and Bill Kircher, the national director of organizing for the AFL/CIO who came to march with the strikers. Finally, Kircher prevailed and Green ordered a reception readied at Modesto so that a great public welcome was made as the marchers walked wearily into town. This major shift in attitudes greatly encouraged the farm workers. Of even more significance, it began a period of lasting solidarity between Chavez, the farm workers and the leaders of the AFL/CIO.

Two days later, as the farm workers marched into Stockton, Cesar received a call from Schenley's counsel offering to recognize the union and sign a contract. After a hurried meeting in San Francisco to finalize this offer, the march continued to Sacramento where they were met by 10,000 people who had gathered on the capitol steps to greet the jubilant, though footsore and weary marchers. Governor Pat Brown was conspicuously absent from the celebratory rally which followed—complete with speeches, songs and a mass. He was still ambivalent about the movement and its political effects at that time, even though he later overcame this reluctance and became a supporter of Chavez and the farm workers.

Although the pilgrimage arose out of the anger against the Shenley violence and utter disregard for workers' health, it became more than just a response to the specific action for it dramatically highlighted the issue of the grape strike. By taking the case to the seat of state government as well as to the public, the legislators and the govenor, *La Causa*, as exemplified by the pilgrimage to Sacramento, impacted other farm workers outside the Delano area.

For Chavez, spiritual values were of major importance. The discipline of the march tested the strikers' endurance for the long, hard struggle ahead. Not only did the marchers' physical fitness and spiritual strength grow, but the pilgrimage also ogave Chavez and the *huelguistas* an opportunity to demonstrate nonviolent action, build public confidence and stress visibly the value of nonviolent tactics. Beyond this we can never underestimate the value of the firm growth in solidarity which developed between the two striking groups—Chavez' N.F.W.A and the AFL/CIO's A.W.O.C.

Kircher, by bringing the AFL/CIO unions into a new supportive relationship with the farm workers, opened up a new era of cooperation. Soon union members throughout the U.S. and Canada gave the rallying cry, "Support our farm worker brothers and sisters." Visits to Forty Acres, the farm worker union's new headquarters in Delano, soon were common occurrences for union members and delegations from unions nationwide. These visits also strengthened the bonds forged on the march. Visits by national union leaders, notably Walter Reuther, made further headlines as, publicly, these ties were cemented. Many unions began to donate substantial funds to the cause.

The Fast

Another unique tactic which Chavez undertook on a number of occasions was a "water or fruit juice" fast. Essentially religious in its motive, the fast was another factor in this unique labor movement which grew out of Cesars' religious and cultural background and which he employed both for his own spirit and for the spiritual needs of his followers. Although sceptics publically doubted his sincerity, those closest to him were convinced that he undertook each of his fasts for a specific, important purpose.

Chavez' most famous fast, which lasted 25 days from February 15th to March 10th, 1968, came at a time when he felt the nonviolent discipline among union members had weakened. Some of the strikers, due to the attacks and harassment from the growers and their hired strikebreakers, wanted to retaliate with counterforce.

Cesar once explained, "The fast is a very personal spiritual thing, and it is not done out of recklessness. It's not done out of a desire to destroy myself but is done out of a deep conviction that we can communicate to people, either those who are against us or for us, faster and more effectively, spiritually, than we can in any other way."

Chavez fasted as both a call to sacrifice for justice and as a reminder of how much suffering there is among farm workers. Even though his health suffered, he felt it was worthwhile. In this regard he once said, "The greatest tragedy is not to live and die—as we all must. The greatest gtragedy is for a person to live and die without knowing the satisfaction of giving life to others."

Cesar fasted a number of times. Chris Hartmire and others fasted with him occasionally to show personal solidarity and for the sake of the religious community. Each fast undertaken success-fully increased commitment on the part of union members, staff and supporters. Politically there was usually little immediate ef-fect. The deep spiritual nature of the fasts was often misunderstood by growers and others who saw them, cynically, as publicity stunts or political maneuvers.

Because of the rapidly spreading media publicity concerning *La Huelga*, the boycotts, the pilgrimages, and the fasts, the gen-eral public grew aware of and were touched by the farm worker movement. Throughout history, the public had often seen labor's strikes in terms of violent clashes, not boycotts and religious acts. These differences, displayed by the farm worker movement, com-pelled the middle class public to empathize with the workers on a higher plane rather than just support a group's demand for more money and gave the movement a moral focus and the character of a crusade.

11. A Model for Cooperation

The leadership of the union and the ministry soon came to understand the functions of the great power of agribusiness and the interconnection of agricultural corporations and financial institutions—how they wield and influence political power and have access to a sympathetic press. Realizing how highly organized agribusiness was and how bitterly it would fight their own efforts at organizing, they soon came to know even more deeply the powerlessness of their stoop labor in a modern agricultural empire. Richard R. Niebuhr, writing in the *Christian Century* (1965:1471) said, "If I may use one word to indicate the meaning of the word 'God', it is power. . . The Gospel of Mark is helpful in this respect, particularly the preaching of the Kingdom of God in that Gospel. . . Christ represented as 'the finger of God,' as the peculiar locus of the divine rule, as the [one] who defines the effectiveness of God's power and suffers it consequences."

From the base of its great power, agribusiness, using the most highly developed scientific farming methods and sophisticated management (except for labor relations!) could avail itself of all the levers of society—enjoying a strong, even dominant, position in society. The managers of such a great enterprise could see no reason to change and resisted fiercely any threat to the status quo.

Further, the one mechanism of change open to the farm worker—the legislative process—was essentially closed because the state legislatures, until quite recently, were dominated by farm county legislators which meant the state legislature faithfully followed the agenda of agribusiness.

One lever of change, the pressure of campaign contributions, was clearly out of the question for a union of the poor. This is not to say that there were no sympathetic legislators, but even those who were open to farm worker needs could accomplish litle when they tried to stand against a large majority with opposite views who were loyal to agribusiness interests. The net result was to keep agribusiness needs well taken care of, while the voice of the work force was stilled.

The average church person is often naive and unsophisticated in understanding the dynamics of power in society. Further, such persons often feel that the use of power, especially political power, is a dirty, unfit enterprise for the church, much less for an individual, especially a religious one. Few hold the view that the use of power can be ethically sound and that power, per se, is neutral.

The leadership of the Migrant Ministry and the farm worker union rightly saw the ability to use power in society as the necessary means to achieve justice. The Biblical view of power condemns its use for corrupt, self-serving purposes. In fact, the prophetic call to righteousness is addressed to political rulers who were abusers of power and is an attempt to redeem them, calling them to righteousness. Warnings given to these community leaders of the dire fate of the corrupt social order were coupled with exhortations to do justly, to walk with God, that is, acting as God acted, and to be faithful to God's commandments.

The change in orientation of the ministry from advocacy to servanthood resulted from the Migrant Ministry's insights in theology, politics and economics—many of which had been gained through living closely with farm worker's leaders and experiencing their struggles for self-determination. The Migrant Ministry acted as a laboratory for mission stategy development, theology-in-action, church deployment of resources and radical social change. The union and ministry, working together in close cooperation, experienced parallel development and growth of understanding in their task and methods.

The importance of this cooperative, shared life, and the mutual understandings gained thereby cannot be over emphasized since this solidarity was essential for the realization of a true servanthood ministry. Already close bonds of friendship and shared purpose had developed between the ministry staff and Cesar Chavez during the community organization training. These bonds were strengthened as the N.F.W.A. was organized and grew, eventually to become the U.F.W. Chavez and Hartmire spent many hours together. Their discussions and concerns focused primarily on developing ways for the Migrant Ministry to serve the union.

Jim Drake, at the Tulare County Community Development Project, became another example of this cooperative relationship for he was able to put himself, his car and his mimeograph machine at the disposal of the union in Porterville. Out of this experience Drake conceived of the worker-minister team program as a primary linkage between the faith community and the union. Good communication existed because the worker-minister relationship easily facilitated the transmission of authentic information. It was a mechanism involving trust, mutual support of the most direct kind and a sharing of experience in the everyday, real world.

Selection and training of worker-minister personnel was most carefully done and involved both Chavez, Hartmire and their staffs. In addition, an advisory committee for the worker-minister program was created. Though small, to facilitate close communication, it included outstanding persons from church and union who carefully monitored the growth of the concept and its implementation.

Although an enduring bond developed between Chavez and Hartmire and their relationship played a major role in the alliance of the farm workers and the faith community, it should not be inferred that successful, faithful mission depends on personal relationships.

Hartmire, a person who never said, "No," when the Migrant Ministry was called upon, was fully committed, even to the point of being jailed with farm workers many times. His truly Christian spirit brought to the relationship with Chavez a dependability that formed the cement of their bond. Though they were quite different in many ways Chavez soon knew he could depend absolutely on Hartmire and the California Migrant Ministry.

Chavez and Hartmire shared many human qualities which formed the core of their strong and enduring friendship. Of course there also existed cultural differences between them, the result of their widely different backgrounds. Yet these differences were not in fundamental areas of belief or value system and were offset by important mutually held attributes.

1. A deep religious commitment to and an awareness of the Christian understanding of social activism and the resulting change. Probably the single most important attribute these two share is this religious commitment and their vital, faith-motivated life. Coming from different races, educational backgrounds, economic classes and experiences they yet had this one factor of faith—though one is Catholic, the other Protestant—which essentially bound them together in their common lifetime struggle. Hartmire did not come to his commitment to enter the Christian ministry until the fourth year of college, while Chavez knew his faith from earliest life, yet faith provided the dominant motivation of life for both.

2. A gentle nature and manner coupled with toughness of purpose, principle and perseverance. This combination of gentle manner and inner toughness was crucial to each when confronted by a hostile audience or when addressing extremely difficult issues. A high degree of disarming candor kept each of them from being abrasive in these confrontations even though they held their ground with great tenacity and were able to maintain it in the face of strong, sometimes angry, resistance.

This characteristic was especially necessary for Hartmire since a major part of his time was spent in interpreting the farm worker cause to church audiences. Many of the things he had to say were unfamiliar, and often unacceptable, to the average church member. His personal charm and nonthreatening manner, coupled with his calm assurance and knowledge of his subject, made him credible and therefore persuasive for many of his hearers.

3. The ability to lead within one's constituency and charismatic communication skills. Being attractive, warmly personable and yet deeply convicted of the rightness of one's cause, makes for effective communication. Hartmire and Chavez combined

these attributes with a sense of mission and each developed outstanding leadership within their constituencies.

Repeatedly, Chavez was able to recruit college students for volunteer work, to establish supportive relationships with industrial union leaders or enlist support in the church community. More importantly, his relationship with the Spanish speaking men who were part of the movement created in them a strong new male image. He challenged them with a new understanding of the meaning of "manhood." Chavez called them to stand up for the right, to give themselves to the nonviolent struggle for justice and to sacrifice for a better life for their kids and family. This truly remarkable message to Mexican men brought a devoted response in them.

Hartmire also experienced widespread positive response to his efforts at creating solidarity in the middle class faith community. Although he met resistance to his message at almost every level of the church, his credibility as a person and his strong commitment presented his hearers with a compelling message that was hard to resist.

4. The belief that the church, in an ecumenical age, had a commitment to social justice. It would be a mistake to underestimate the role of the ecumenical spirit of the 1960s as a supportive climate for the farm worker movement. In 1962 Pope John 23 convened Vatican II and a "breath of fresh air" blew through the whole Roman church. Robert McAfee Brown, who served as a Protestant observer at Vatican II in Rome, cites an example of the effect of this on farm workers. A few days after returning to California from the last council session, Brown was able to speak at a farm worker strike meeting in Delano, reporting directly from the assembly of Catholic cardinals and bishops who had just completed a long document which reaffirmed the right of workers to organize, to bargain collectively and the moral right to strike. He recalls today, "I was able to read to this mainly Catholic gathering, in the Filipino Hall in Delano, statements that their own church leaders had made just two or three days earlier." In other words the pope and the 2,300 bishops reaffirmed the things that these people had been struggling to achieve for many years!

It had an immediate, profound impact.

Vatican II, taking action half way round the world, confirmed in the minds of Chavez and Hartmire that in an ecumenical age the church did have a commitment to its mandate for justice and social change. The mainline Protestant churches also gave evidence of this commitment.

5. A celebratory spirit—even in adversity. This attribute of the Christian faith, shared by these two men of faith, was very much a part of the living out of their faith. Neither used their religion in a manipulative or strategic way—it was simply the natural outgrowth of their faith. For Cesar it was completely natural to have a mass at a public rally or to march with Protestants, Jews and Catholics—all under the banner of the Virgin of Guadalupe. This natural expression of faith was authentic and communicated itself powerfully to leaders and the public.

6. An understanding and acceptance of the role of servant-leader. Both Chavez and Hartmire accepted this role in contrast with the prevailing American myth of the fearless, bold leader in the tradition of Teddy Roosevelt. Both also held to this servant aspect of their self-image as they worked together to build the union and lead the churches into an alliance with it. The basic source of this self-understanding is, of course, the life and ministry of Jesus Christ, the suffering servant. There was also, in the case of Hartmire, the conscious acceptance of the theology of mission developed by the commission of the California Migrant Ministry.

The authentic servant leader of a movement of poor people accepts poverty and personal sacrifice as essential. Cesar, born into poverty, might have been expected to pursue riches as soon as possible. However, in assuming the leadership of a group of poor people, he instinctively knew that they could achieve self-determination only through sacrifice, so he consciously turned away from the more traditional control technique of using money for the power it could bring and sought instead to create power for his people through organization, appeal to public conscience and the practice of sacrificial dedication to the cause. As Cesar often said, "All we have is our lives."

7. The subsistence life-style—source of strength. Because

farm workers perforce subsist at the poverty level Chavez insisted upon payment of only "bare living expenses plus $5 per week" for himself and called upon the other union personnel and the volunteers working with the union to accept it also. Knowing that union members and leaders had committed themselves to subsistence living became a powerful motivator for many of the idealistic middle class volunteers who joined the movement.

Growers and the general public had much difficulty comprehending this acceptance of a poverty life-style at the top of the union. It was a rare phenomenon in American labor. The subsistence life-style, when one considers its ramifications for the church hierarchy and the executives of social change movements, constitutes a revolutionary notion.

8. Humility, imagination, creativity and tenacity. Hartmire and Chavez shared these traits and each has developed his effectiveness with tenacious drive. Their imagination and creativity was responsible for their ability to adapt to rapidly changing situations. When faced with the power of the growers and their clever tactics, the union was forced to use strategic responses, often brilliantly. The pilgrimage exemplifies creative leadership. A major effect of the pilgrimages was increased public awareness. However, it was undertaken at a time when most farm workers were unable to work. Therefore, through this march to Sacramento, Chavez gave them meaningful activity which also benefited the cause. Likewise the boycotts were begun because the strike alone could not have succeeded.

9. Ability to create guilt in persons of conscience. Perhaps least recognized among Christian virtues is the ability to make persons of conscience feel guilty and change their behaviour. While not used by Chavez and Hartmire as a conscious manipulative technique, their words often resulted in guilt feelings on the part of those who heard them. It may well have been a product of their sense of mission, their dedication and utter sincerity, but its effect was generally productive of a motivational response.

10. Trust, in each other and of others in them. Soon after Hartmire and Chavez met a strong sense of mutual trust developed between them which grew through the mutual experiences, trials

and sacrifices of their work together. They were each able to elicit trust in others, leading people to trust both of them and their mission. This quality in Chavez was immediately apparent to church leaders meeting him. Likewise farm workers coming to church meetings with Chavez or Hartmire created feelings of trust as they, though often ill at ease, were wholly convinced of the justice of their movement.

11. Ability to learn through mistakes. That mistakes occurred as the movement developed should not be a surprise. Constantly changing dynamics, tactics and actions, using media and other forms of communication, were made in response to problems as they arose. Far from causing despair mistakes usually turn out to be learning experiences. For example, the union's dues structure from the beginning had been set at $3.50 per month, every month, even if not working. This was too great a burden for some and the membership suffered. With the signing of the first contract, Chavez changed the dues to two percent of one's monthly earnings. This everyone could handle and as wage increases were won the union's income increased accordingly.

12. Strength through discipline—a religious tool. One of the most striking aspects of Chavez' character is his great discipline—something he clearly demonstrated in the several fasts he undertook. For Chavez the fast is deeply rooted in religious convictions, although he also was strongly influenced by Ghandi's fasts which he studied from the time he first learned about Ghandi through a 1930s newsreel. Chavez' fasts were always religious, but they had the direct effect of stengthening the movement. The first major fast was taken during a time of severe testing and served to reinforce the union's commitment to nonviolence.

Clearly, fasting was a personal religious act for Chavez, made public for the sake of his fellow farm workers. Much of the public, including many growers, saw it—at best—as a tactical ploy or—at worst—as a publicity stunt. They could not understand its religious nature, especially in the context of a good old American labor strike.

Examples of discipline in Chavez' management of the union abound. He deeply believed that he could not accept a large salary while farm workers lived in poverty. He instituted subsistence salaries for himself and other union leaders. Often he had to struggle to maintain this plan against strong internal criticism. He never wavered. Also, in the spring of 1968, when good management practice called for development of the institution, he sent everyone out to work in the boycott and concentrated on winning, instead of building a bureaucracy.

This discussion of the similarities of character between Chavez and Hartmire should not be seen to set rigid criteria for all situations. Each ministry will have its own inner logic in personnel matters as well as in other aspects of its life. It is hard to see how a shared ministry could be built without Christian commitment and dedication, without common understanding of the society in which it will function and without shared goals for mission.

12. Migrant Ministry Documents

"God purposes a good life for all [people]. From the beginning he has worked toward this goal. From the beginning he has been willing to join humanity in the working out of this purpose and in so doing he has described and lived out the content of this full life, this 'saved' life. . . . God chose Israel, his people. . . . Justice was to be the framework, the structure of their corporate life.

"The Migrant Ministry seeks to gather the people of God in their scattered situation into an interdenominational program of service. Professional staff people needle and lead these folks, but we are not the Migrant Ministry, we, *together with* the scattered people in service, are the Migrant Ministry. In communities where this happens, the Migrant Ministry is a ministry *of* the church *to* the people of the world. . . . We are then also a ministry *to* the church for the *sake* of the world."

So begins the *The Migrant Ministry and the Mission of the Church*—which is a collection of 41 California Migrant Ministry (C.M.M.) documents. They were produced because Chris Hartmire wanted to develop an authentic theology of mission which would be the basis for the Migrant Ministry. They were used to stimulate in-depth, theological discussions of pertinent issues and events facing the C.M.M. and to help define their unique ministry to farm workers. These became important tools for the commission members that helped them focus their some-what divergent views of theology and sociology. Through pro-longed discussions the commission members managed to achieve a degree of understanding of their leadership role in this ministry to farm workers.

The documents can be organized into four categories:

I. Theology, Goals and Objectives: Documents Nos. 1, 2, 3, and 4 developed the theological framework of the ministry and led up to No. 5 which defined the goals and objectives for a servanthood ministry among farm workers.

II. Strategy and Program Development: Documents Nos. 6, 7, 8, 9, 11, 13, 15, 27 and 28 contain policy statements and plans for program development to implement the theology and goals laid out in document No. 5.

III. Interpretation Evaluation and Action: Documents Nos. 10, 12, 14, 16, 17, 18, 19, 32, 34, 37 and 38 are interpretative pieces whereas Nos. 20, 21, 22, 23, 24, 25, 26, 29, 30 and 31 contain evaluation in contrast to Nos. 33, 35 and 36 which elicit action.

IV. Transition—N.M.M. to N.F.W.M.: Documents Nos. 39, 40, 41, written between January and May, 1971, deal with the transition—with help of C.M.M.—from the National Migrant Ministry to the National Farm Worker Ministry. During this transition period in 1971 when the National Farm Worker Ministry succeeded the National Migrant Ministry, the California Migrant Ministry made available to the new organization its director and staff along with its financial resources. This effectively transferred to a national body the alliance existing between the United Farm Worker Union and the California ministry. The churches' structure now matched the expected national scope of the union. The C.M.M., after a period of supportive relationship, became inoperative except as a communication link and the N.F.W.M., which affiliated with the National Council of Churches, continued the church wide expression of solidarity with farm workers.

Utilizing a conscious process and facing social issues in a theological context, as the Migrant Ministry did in this instance, gives to any group serving the poor an authentic, solid base for mission. This involves analyzing, from the farm workers' point of view, their real-life issues—even to the extent of participating with them in their struggles. This methodology was, in short, a planned action for social change combined with theological reflection. It is no wonder that authentic Christian mission developed in the context of this direct relationship with the suffering persons.

To achieve an authentic servanthood ministry requires study, group dynamics, action and reflection. Particular circumstances, of course, determine specific forms to be used, but these general elements apply in all such endeavors. This course of action, used by the Migrant Ministry to organize its action/reflection operating methods, contains lessons for all who would engage in social change ministry.

The state commission was given primary responsibility for policy and oversight of the Migrant Ministry's program. During its thrice-yearly meetings, generally in February, May and October, the full commission of 30 members considered these issues. Between each of these meetings the commission's executive committee (composed of the commission's elected officers, chairpersons and two or three at large members—about ten people in all) met to plan program and deal with the current issues of policy, tactics and administration.

The staff scheduled most meetings in locations where the farm worker union had some action underway. Commission members thus could participate in various aspects of the union's activities during the two days of the meeting. This involvement might include taking a turn at serving on the picket line, meeting with the generally hostile law enforcement officials, or discovering the local perspectives by engaging in dialogue with city officials, growers, business people, nonunion farm workers or other interested observers. These meetings took place in such sensitive sites as Delano, Fresno, Bakersfield, Porterville or Calexico.

In Delano the commission usually arranged their schedule so they could attend the Friday night strike meetings at the Philippino Hall. Here they would hear reports from the picket lines, strategy discussions and other union business. Often Cesar and other union officers addressed these meetings.

Through this direct participation with what was happening

in the fields, commission members experienced firsthand the democratic workings of the union, observing many *Huelga* events as they occurred. Attending these meetings also provided the commission members, who for the most part came from the middle class, an authentic foundation of experience for their study and theological reflection.

Director Hartmire frequently consulted with the commission chairperson, the council executives and members of the executive committee as these various documents were being prepared. He wrote most of the documents that were produced between February 1963 and February 1971, although sometimes with staff or commission member help. Each one was drafted to meet a specific purpose.

These papers were normally distrubuted by Hartmire at the commission meetings where a variety of group dynamic methods were used to discuss, analyze and revise these papers. Long hours of hard intellectual and spiritual work occurred before a document was finalized. Often, the work was divided and given to smaller groups of members for more detailed discussion on particular points. Then it would be brought back to the whole group which would have another go at it. Thoughtful positions, policies and actions resulted from this procedure.

Discussion and debate regarding the issues in these documents often were emotionally loaded and heated. Since commission members came from many diverse backgrounds, usually including a few small growers whose natural inclination was to side with agribusiness, their points of view often clashed. This give and take was enlightening to all sides.

Fortunately, though some of the commission members empathized more with the workers while others tended to side with the growers, all members came with a strong commitment to a Christian ministry among farm workers. This dedication gave them all an impetus to work through the tough problems, such as the decision to stand firm with the workers when they clearly indicated that a union was their goal. A strong personal bond soon developed in the group as they pursued this process. Further, having worked together so intensely, each member felt an ownership in the final result.

Most commission members were on the board representing a particular denomination or church organization. Thus the body of studies and the resulting documentation discussed herein formed a rich, valid eye-witness basis for subsequent reports and interpretation made to the members' constituencies.

As the controversy widened to the whole church, the need for interpretation increased. The staff, with their limited time, met the demand for speakers by turning to the commission members who made numerous presentations to a wide variety of groups—religious and secular. Open discussion on these occasions often became heated but this only helped the commission members to develop great forensic skills in order to survive in the process of meeting their hearers' often-angry objections, prejudices and misunderstandings.

One person whose dedicated service was essential to the effectiveness of the Migrant Ministry, and to the ongoing task of the documentation outlined here, was Sue Miner. Joining the California Migrant Ministry in 1955 when it was under the guidance of Dean Collins she served him and three subsequent directors as an effective and efficient administrative assistant until her retirement in December of 1983. Not only was she honored at the celebration of the Ministry's 60th Anniversary—and her 25th year of service—but also at her retirement three years later. At that function Fred Ross, Sr., reminisced, "While others surged in and out the front, side and back doors past her room in the Los Angeles office, Sue was methodically gathering all the loose ends together, always calm in the midst of general pandemonium, strong and firm and sure, ready to help, to offer a sturdy shoulder for us to sob on, or a steady hand to hold, and welcoming arms."

Sue Miner's commitment and devotion to *La Causa* served as an inspiration to countless persons who came to support, in any way, the farm workers ministry. She attended all board and most committee meetings, providing administrative support and continuity. Her steadfastness over the 28 years of her service exemplifies the highest level of servanthood and to her credit these important documents were drafted and crafted with care so

that they could influence the wide audience they have reached.
An examination of several of these documents, by which
the California Migrant Ministry determined the theological and
sociological framework for its ministry among farm workers,
gives us insight into the thoroughness used by the director and
commission members to produce this model methodology.

I. Theology, Goals and Objectives

Documents One through Four make up the study papers used
by Hartmire to stimulate the commission to discuss servanthood
ministry among farm workers. Each study paper opened with
reflections—theological, Biblical and sociological—-followed by
thought provoking questions on the pertinent issues. The resultant
discussions were lively and often heated. The commission usually
was able to achieve consensus on most issues.

The first four documents, presented at the three commission
meetings during 1963 and at a staff meeting in December 1963,
helped to clarify and unify the concepts held by the commission
members and staff, and finally resulted in the fifth document,
"Goals for California Migrant Ministry." There followed a
thorough process of discussion and revision of the document by
the commission and it was submitted to the California Church
Council which formally adopted it on March 5, 1964.

Exerpts from these specific papers include:

1. *The Migrant Ministry and the Mission of the Church*,
February 1963. "The church as gathered, visible community exists
so that people may learn how to trust and forgive and depend on
one another. . . This witness to full life is incomplete if [it is]
not extended into the world around the gathered community.
There is no full life for an elite. The gathered community exists
to train people to live full lives . . . Life in the community is
incomplete, not full. . . It is preparation for the full life. There
is necessary interaction between life-together and life-in-the-
world. . . The latter depends for its fullness on the former, as
do nurture and worship."

Some of the discussion questions which followed were:

1). What is the nature of the church's institutional ministry? What forms does this collective ministry take? Pronouncements? Political action? 2. Given this moment in history, what is our first priority task? Does a full, effective ministry among workers "prepare the way" for the institutional church's outreach? 3. Does full life depend upon participation in a local expression of the church? If yes, what is the validity of our non- institutional efforts in fringes and camps?

2. *Being Used on the Rural Fringe*, May 1963, explores the theological foundation for servanthood, citing Jesus as the paradigm of servant. The world "uses" Christ for its salvation whereas the Christian community, if it to deserve his name, lives a life of servanthood and is thus "being used" by persons in need.

"Only as we unite our various gifts are we able to be 'used' (as Jesus was) by people for redemption. . . . Denominations and local congregations are called to be 'used' by persons for any purpose. . . . The Christan community should strain toward full servanthood. It is hard to be 'used' by people. Indeed we sometimes positively evaluate our work on the basis of having escaped 'being used'. Yet radical servanthood is 'being used' by persons. Individuals, denominations and local congregations are called to be used by people. . . . I propose we encourage a full servant ministry in a rural fringe."

Questions regarding the servanthood ministry included:

1). Can it be done a better way?

2). Who would sponsor it?

3). Is such a ministry possible in an ethnically diverse low, income area?

4). Is the theological statement on servanthood close to adequate?

5). In terms of priorities, are we better off investing time and energy in existing projects to increase their effectiveness rather than proposing an additional enterprise?

3. *Questions Related to "Love and Justice"*, The commission met in September 1963 and explored the relationship between love and justice using a question format. The discussions centered on the relevance of these questions for church social action and the church's role in raising these ethical issues. Some of the questions explored were:

1). How is Jesus a norm for love lived out?

2). Is justice a useful category only in social group relations, balancing or limiting demands of competing power groups?

3). Is the cry of the oppressed for justice distinct from the basic human cry for the nourishment of love? How are these yearnings related?

4). Is love a relevant basis for ethical activity in the social realm?

5). Was Jesus' "attack" on the Pharisees an act of love? Is the Migrant Ministry's "attack" on certain growers an act of love?

After the fight to eliminate the *bracero* program was waged in 1964, the Migrant Ministry struggled with the question of its ministry to small farmers. "Are we against them? Doesn't God's love include them? What is the meaning of love and justice as they apply to the Migrant Ministry and these small growers?" This paper initiated a subject which became a subject of continuing discussion and the effort to deal with this issue continues until today.

Quoting H. Richard Niebuhr's statement that the church's purpose is to facilitate "The increase among [persons] of the love of God and neighbor," the paper ended with a final question, "Is it possible to identify with the beloved and their community (rich *or* poor) without dealing with issues of justice and injustice for those beloveds in their families, in their social groups and in their society at large?"

4. *Where is the Migrant Ministry Going?* The commission discussed this theme in November 1963 and examined some priority tasks, notable among them:

Help farm workers and other fringe residents find dignity in a struggle of their own for equality of participation and opportunity through

1). Community development projects and training,

2). Inclusion of farm workers at all levels of Migrant Ministry planning and other agency planning and

3). See this struggle for what it means to farm workers and

our kind of church members. For the latter it may be a necessary attack on the cancer of arrogance.

5. *Goals for the Migrant Ministry,* developed by the staff and commission during this time period, opened with a brief theological statement, "The California Migrant Ministry exists to bring to life among seasonal farm workers and their neighbors this Good News of a merciful and just God who is Lord of history and who purposed that his children shall know forgiveness and new life in Jesus Christ and shall live together in mutual relationships of respect, understanding, concrete concern and joint enterprise."

There followed a section on objectives which listed specific types of mission targeted on four distinct groups: 1). Seasonal farm workers, their families and organizations; 2). Christian organizations; 3) Agricultural employers and their organizations; and 4) Community groups, public agencies, legislators and others. This document concluded with a section of program outlines for each of the four identified groups. This thorough planning document was the basic policy guide for the C.M.M. over the next several years.

These first five documents provide a corpus of evidence showing the development of a complete theological and programmatic foundation for the life and actions of the C.M.M. and which demonstrate this rare example of painstaking planning for "Christian Action." These documents remain for us today as a model process for persons of faith who seek to be effective "servants of the least of these."

A key to the theological maturity of the authors of the document is found in this affirmation, "We will give strongest support to those actions which strengthen the ability of farm workers to identify and deal with their own problems."

II. Strategy and Program Development

A number of subsequent Migrant Ministry documents which emerged from the commission discussions concentrated on proposals for program development. The most significant of them deal with strategy and program ideas which generally originated with the staff although commission members reviewed and modified these proposals before authorizing final action. Many members of the commission had professional responsibility for mission development and administration and their expertise and creativity figured importantly in developing the ministry program.

One underlying assumption throughout this study testifies to the crucial link that the Migrant Ministry served between the middle class—especially in the churches—and the farm worker community, which comprised the union. It was this linkage which provided the stimulus to responsive ministry and servanthood on the part of many otherwise apathetic churchgoers. Over and over these documents remind us that "The problem of our time is the *gap* between verbal identity with Christ and concrete deeds that reflect his identification with human suffering."

These papers document the strategy which evolved making the primary message of the Migrant Ministry a call to the churches to accept servanthood and advocacy as their mission methodology. Thus the major program proposals outlined in the following documents demonstrate this philosophy:

8. The California Migrant Ministry and the Economic Opportunity Act of 1964 (E.O.A.), issued in June 1965, examined the E.O.A. and its possible relation to the plight of the farm workers It explained why the Migrant Ministry's acceptance of grants from the E.O.A.'s implementing agency, the Office of Economic Opportunity (O.E.O.), might prostitute its concept of redressing the power balance between workers and growers. The commission accepted this analysis and refused to seek such contracts for the C.M.M. to operate O.E.O. programs.

In spite of this the O.E.O. actively sought out Migrant Ministry sponsorship in several states, as in Arizona, because they sought contracts with well established groups who had valid track records and acceptance among farm workers.

The California Migrant Ministry, based upon its Tulare County experience, saw several pitfalls in using these programs. Not only could the farm worker leadership and the staff of the Migrant Ministry, as sponsors, become bogged down in detail and lose sight of the real justice struggle, but they also could become totally absorbed in grant writing and reporting activity—thus losing program direction. The threat of governmental pressure or control might also prejudice the ministry's independence of thought and action. The O.E.O., by its very nature, lacked the freedom to support militant community organizing. Thus, in effect, a Migrant Ministry as an O.E.O. contractor would be forced into thwarting self-determination for farm workers—a denial of its mandate.

The Migrant Ministry thus percieved the O.E.O., with its generous grants—though beguiling—as a roadblock instead of a positive force in its all-out war on poverty. Experience bore out the truth of the C.M.M. staff assessment that the O.E.O. would offer just enough hope to keep oppressed people from necessary militant action, buying off just those people and agencies who otherwise would have joined in and supported such actions.

However, it was this study of an alternate form of ministry that served to strengthen the C.M.M.'s resolve to pursue its own servanthood ministry. The concluding statement of this rather pessimistic document clearly stated the essence of the objections to O.E.O. contracts since an alliance with the government might "strengthen and prolong the widespread myth that the problem is primarily in the people who are poor and not in an unjust social order that is *our* responsibility."

This document, along with a letter to Dr. Shirley Greene, an N.C.C.C. official, urged that, based on this analysis, some of the funds and staff slated for work with the "War on Poverty" be channeled into "a relentless, full-time, nationwide lobbying effort for extension of bargaining rights and minimum wage to farm workers and all laborers." This sage advice, unfortunately, went unheeded.

11. *Christian Action with Farm Workers,* issued in September 1965, was a document calling for an alternate migrant ministry "to establish an independent, nonprofit Christian action group to assist farm workers with basic grass roots organization."

Following the strike in Delano, Hartmire, Drake, and a few others, foresaw severe crises arising in the days ahead. As a fallback alternative they proposed a noninstitutional method of continuing the servanthood ministry should the councils and churches prove unable to stick it out with the Migrant Ministry and the farm workers union. At that time these leaders gave the churches about a 60 percent chance of staying with them in the struggle. Later they would have to admit they had underestimated both the intensity of the controversy and the courage and solidarity of the friends of farm workers in the denominations and local churches. Fortunately, this solidarity on the part of many individuals and church bodies meant this contingency plan never was put into effect.

15. Farm Worker-Ministers, A Proposal to the Churches, December 1965. The Farm Worker-Minister program proposal was accepted by the California Church Council at this time and further Documents in this series—22, 24 and 25—contain reports on the progress of this program which defined the central role played by C.M.M. in solidarity with the U.F.W.

27. Proposal for an Expanded Ecumenical Ministry to the Farm Workers' Movement, February 2, 1968. This document, which was approved by the California Church Council as determining C.M.M.'s program direction, included an update and history of the farm worker struggle along with an assessment of the current situation. It was felt that the church's involvement in the strike had reached a dangerous point since interest in the strike had fallen off in urban areas and concluded that the possibility of a significant Christian presence and influence was dependent on decisions that would be made in 1968. With this prediction and warning, Hartmire outlined the importance of continued church involvement, proposing major program thrusts through an expanded Farm Worker-Minister program and an ecumenical ministry to the strike community in the Delano area with anticipated Roman Catholic participation.

28. The Churches and the Continuing Farm Worker Struggle, issued June 8, 1968, was a call to action addressed to the denominations asking for a continuing support of the strike and the giving of leadership in rural churches to bring about social change. The denominations were also asked to use their good offices to urge employers to bargain with workers and seek to extend the provisions of the National Labor Relations Act to farm workers which would guarantee their rights to fair labor practices currently denied them.

III. Interpretation, Evaluation and Action

The next 24 documents in this series fall under three headings in purpose and content. Eleven of them (Nos. 10, 12, 14, 16, 17, 18, 19, 32, 34, 37, and 38) serve as interpretive papers. Usually directed to the churches-the specific constituency of the C.M.M.—they answered the major questions in the minds of concerned people. Ten of these documents (Nos. 20 through 26, 29, 30 and 31) evaluated specific aspects of the events and showed the careful process of program review which was followed by the staff and the commission. Three of the papers (Nos. 33, 35 and 36) called churches and their members to action while specifically identifying the rationale and need for this requested actions. Statements of support by church leaders, the California Church Council, C.M.M. and its constituent judicatories comprise five of the documents (Nos. 10, 14, 16, 17 and 18). The director's reports to the state commission make up an additional 14 documents (Nos. 12, 16, 17, 19, 21, 22, 24, 25, 26, 30, 31, 32, 34, and 37).

20. *Report—Student Summer Program* was an extensive staff report of the 1966 summer program which was sponsored by the N.F.W.A. instead of the C.M.M., details the first time use of cosponsors. Also involved in this summer project were the Student Nonviolent Coordinating Committee (S.N.C.C.), the National Student Association, the National Student Christian Federation, the Young Christian Students and the Students for a Democratic Society (S.D.S.).

Through this unique collection of agencies, word about the Migrant Ministry and the union's alliance went out far and wide. Recruitment efforts included mailings through the National Student Association to every college student in school government, to the National Student Christian Federation roster, to every

United Church of Christ and Methodist campus pastor and to strike support groups.

Soon displays and posters calling for volunteers could be seen at colleges throughout California. Student papers printed interviews with those involved and speeches were made at events on over 20 California colleges campuses. Some 120 students wrote inquiring about the internship program and some some 80 made firm commitments to attend at least an orientation session. Of these, 50 students remained throughout the summer and later another ten joined the movement. Even after school was back in session some 25 students remained with the strike until November 1st.

It is no wonder that the evaluation report states, "The student 'shock troops' with their militancy, freedom from niceties of protocol, and time pressure of wanting immediate results were very effective in the boycott."

From 1966 through 1969 the C.M.M. was able to create a widespread network of supporters. The regular channels of the major denominations provided easy access to church officials and, through them, to parishes. These avenues became the most often used channels for interpretation and calls to action. In addition, a mailing list of several hundred names, referred to as the "Action Mailing List", provided a quick mobilization network of committed individuals.

The Orange County (California) Interfaith Committee to Aid Farm Workers was outstanding among the several support groups formed around the country. Led by Jeanne Giordano—and later her lawyer husband, Roy—hundreds of supporters responded to her dedicated leadership over 20 years of persistent faithfulness. She produced a newsletter, organized picket lines, contacted the press, promoted among local parishes the annual Farm Worker Week and carried out fund raising events—often at their home in Corona del Mar. Members of the union still find her home not only a base of operations in Southern California, but often a haven from the strain of union activities. In recent years she has joined the National Farm Worker Ministry staff as a worker-minister, yet continues the support group.

College students, and other young people, often acted as catalysts bringing together migrant workers and urban church folk so that they became not only well acquainted but were comfortable being with one another. One student at the University of California, Irvine—Baldwin Keenan—who was one of the first organizers in Orange County, called on Jean and Frank Forbath to tell them of the grape boycott. In response to this call Frank, an engineer, and Jean gathered their seven children and were soon passing out leaflets urging shoppers at supermarkets throughout the area to support farm workers by boycotting table grapes. The entire Forbath family, with the youngest in her carriage, made quite an impressive sight.

After doing this dozens of times they became more involved in the grape boycott and took particular pleasure, when leafletting, in meeting friends—some of whom lacked understanding or sympathy for the farm worker cause. Before long the news of the Forbaths' dedication to *La Causa* reached Delano and, not surprisingly, when Chavez led a pilgrimage along the coast to defeat Proposition 22 (A California Farm Bureau initiative aimed at restricting the farm workers) he and others with him were welcomed into the home of these dependable supporters. Later they joined the 25 to 40 persons who walked with him and helped to defeat the measure, 59 percent to 41 percent. Thus did this middle class family become committed allies in the campesino struggle for justice.

The remaining documents in this series cover various activities and stress the five injunctions the commission felt to be crucial to the church's faithful involvement: 1). Maintain a strong presence with the union, 2). Maintain the Worker-Minister program, 3). Maintain the summer program, 4). Maintain contact with the rural fringe projects and 5). Provide continual interpretation to the denominations.

IV. Transition—National Farm Worker Ministry Established

The documents in this section, especially Nos. 39, 40 and 41, deal with the origins and working rules of the National Farm

Worker Ministry and the transition process by which the C.M.M. made available its staff and financial resources to this new national agency which was affiliated with the National Council of Churches.

Summary

This body of carefully thought-out theological interpretation, mission strategy, evaluation and action statements are crucial to understanding Christian mission as it was developed and lived out by the California Migrant Ministry. The result of many hours of labor by committed Christians approaching their servanthood ministry with devotion and skill, these documents exemplify the Migrant Ministry's intentional self-understanding—reached through a conscious search. Such a thorough exercise of this caliber is usually lacking in most efforts at social change. Excerpts of these documents were widely read and studied—by the staff and persons involved in the denominational rural fringe ministries, by the farm worker's leadership and the worker-priests, by the members of the state commission, by the several thousand supporters and by denominational persons throughout the country. All tended to use these papers as an invaluable resource for study and interpretation so that they eventually impacted an even greater audience.

The practice of using theological reflection as an integral part of the program of action most significantly provided those involved with an authentic and realistic understanding of the situation of farm workers coupled with a Biblically based theology of mission. Subsequently it has been used as a model for social change under the title, *Action/Reflection Methodology.*

The discipline of committing to writing the insights gained in the process of action/reflection helped guide participants and provided a useful, balanced base of documentation for others. The oft-heard criticism of the social activist as being one-sided is belied by use of this careful, comprehensive method of social analysis and mission strategy development. Both the staff and commission tended to hold a Biblical theology more neoorthodox than liberal and from this foundation the Migrant Ministry created its own theology.

The validation of theology is its materialization in real-life experience with poor, marginal people. It was here, in the theology of the Migrant Ministry, that many parallels can be seen with the emerging Liberation Theology in Latin America. In both situations the church, and its Bible imperatives for justice, came together with the people in their common life. Action sprang from this juxtaposition with vitality and spirit. Faith was the sustaining force in all the sacrifice and struggle. As an agency of the church, the Migrant Ministry had, through the faithful, careful development of a mission strategy, acheived a mature servanthood ministry.

These theological parallels and the nature of the leadership of union and ministry through which this authentic relationship was realized are important among the unique gifts which the Migrant Ministry gave to the church.

13. The Church As Servant

A noted Christian once remarked, "The church exists for mission as fire exists for burning." If the church and its mission are inseparable the first question a Christian community faces when planning mission becomes, "How shall we define our mission? Having defined it, how shall we shape that mission?"

A variety of possibilities exist. A list of essential elements would include an authentic Biblical theology, an accurate analysis of the human condition, the provision of adequate resources, committed persons and a plan of action. The essential quality of such a ministry—servanthood—is best nurtured in the context of Christians sharing life experiences with other people as they seek to develop ministry. Simply put, servanthood means mission *with*, rather than *for* or *to*, oppressed people. It means having sensitivity to their need for dignity, empowerment and self-determination rather than treating them paternalistically as recipients or objects of charity.

Careful formation of the ministry thus emerges as the key issue, at any time, whether for an individual, the local church, an intermediate judicatory, denomination or cooperative agency. In fact, one must first determine which of these entities is the appropriate one for the particular ministry. Whereas individuals can function with great flexibility and freedom, they usually lack resources and therefore effectiveness. The local congregation faces restriction in action due to its need to achieve some degree of consensus. While denominations have the greatest access to resources and may achieve consensus more easily than local churches, they can be frustratingly slow to move, especially on hard issues. The problem of constituency approval of a particular ministry decreases in direct relation to the distance from local control. Interchurch agencies appear to have the most freedom for bold, creative ministry, because, coupled with their direct access to denominational resources, they are relatively independent and thus able to carry on ministry involving difficult and controversial issues.

If one accepts our opening statement, the need to create effective ministries focused on specific human needs becomes paramount. Ideally this should be true at all levels—individual, church, denomination or cooperative agency. However, experience indicates that the lower the level at which the ministry exists, the more bland it must be to avoid disabling divisiveness. It is true that the actions of the Migrant Ministry sparked division in local churches and denominations because its ministry was located in a cooperative interchurch agency. Somewhat removed from local constituencies, it was still able to function with effectiveness. Denominations, local churches and individuals felt free to support it when they agreed with its stance, in spite of vocal opposition.

Those local churches which displayed the best ability to support farm workers openly and aggressively revealed a number of common characteristics. First, and perhaps most importantly, they enjoyed skillful clergy leaders who possessed clear personal convictions, expressed them graciously and helped parishioners learn to disagree with one another yet remain in fellowship. They also managed to maintain a strong pastoral relationship even with those who disagreed.

To be a church-in-mission requires the attributes of clear preaching and teaching of the Biblical imperative—to seek justice. Throughout the time of the farm worker struggles, successful leaders showed great skill at presenting the prophetic gospel in the context of personal warmth, spirituality and an authentic concern for persons as well as issues. These clergy presented a wide spectrum of opportunities for self-expression in the church. They helped each person feel accepted and find a place in the total ministry of the church. They forced no one into an untenable position. A sense of community and shared ministry was maintained in this way.

Of course, to reach full realization, clergy leadership requires the partnership of the laity in leadership roles. In the churches engaged in active social ministry, lay persons should be allowed to provide essential functions including decision-making in the conduct of that ministry.

Ralph Kennedy, elder of the First Presbyterian Church of Fullerton, California, showed indefatigable zeal in promoting the farm worker cause at the local, community and presbytery levels. Although the church's pastor, Ralph Haas, also gave active support to the movement, it was Kennedy who led his church's mission in this regard.

Credit must also be given to those lay persons who, unlike Kennedy, lacked clergy support, but still managed to create within their congregations a core of persons dedicated to farm worker solidarity. These groups often worked very quietly but effectively—not clandestinedly, but without forcing the rest of the congregation to accept their position. Keith and Fran Taeger were another notable team who gave effective leadership to the local migrant ministry over many years in the Stockton-Lodi area. These two organized the Stockton Metro Ministry and later gave leadership to the San Joaquin Migrant Ministry.

Deeper understanding and the ability to perform effective ministry are enhanced through one's personal experience. This can best be gained by working in direct relationship alongside suffering people. Many opportunities for the mission enterprise exist for this kind of personal interaction. Those participating in the Migrant Ministry programs—from churches and denominations—built upon these personal experiences and the staff made a conscious effort to facilitate their relationships with the workers.

Farm workers, and later union officials including Chavez, regularly appeared at church gatherings or met with various commission committees. Likewise attendance at farm worker events by clergy and laity provided meaningful contacts and relationships which deepened and grew as people worked together in various local support groups, on picket or boycott lines, or collected and distributed food and supplies.

A person's first awareness of farm worker oppression can

provide a powerful new experience. Few persons can forget their visits to any of the various Migrant Ministry sites in California. As "new" Christians my wife and I made such a visit. Witnessing the harsh working conditions, the deprivation and the discrimination under which the workers lived shocked our generally naive sensibilities. Yet, to our surprise, we found these migrant workers to be people of great courage. In the midst of poverty, disease, malnutrition and pain they were able to remain a beautiful, loving, caring people who only sought to build a good life for their families.

We found sensitivity and warmth and quality of family life among the poorest of the farm workers. Of course not all farm workers are saints. They are basically much the same as other people, yet somehow culture, sacrifice, faith or a combination of these, conditioned them to live, with grace, in a degrading situation. We witnessed an inherent sense of self-worth which would eventually enable them to make the sacrifices to which Cesar Chavez would be forced to call them.

Such personal human contacts with the farm workers influenced many church members and subsequently through them the churches which became the base from which many volunteered to be "servants of farm workers," working within the alliance of the farm workers union and the Migrant Ministry. Of course not everyone understood the theological significance of the term servanthood, but many knew intuitively the dire need of someone to perform the servanthood role, doing everyday deeds with loyal commitment.

And it was through these acts the church became servant, for surely the church of the Suffering Servant will perform as a servant in its mission with the suffering world. Such a church, of necessity, will not be something one goes to, or even serves in, but will be manifest by what it does. It was a struggle for those involved to develop this type of mission in the Migrant Ministry, but it was our mandate.

The Migrant Ministry developed its innovative mission strategies during a time of worldwide ferment in society. Rapid social change, even revolution, was happening in most all the postcolonial countries of the world. This created theological as well as sociological ferment worldwide. It was in this crucible of rapid social change that liberation theology was born in Latin America and the Faith Community-Farm Worker alliance was founded in North America.

There was, at this time, an increase in awareness—a period of rising expectations—among oppressed people, especially as they began hearing the message of the gospel in the words and deeds of Western Christian missionaries. This gospel message comes to life as words are backed up by deeds, and, conversely, when deeds are illumined with words. Then servanthood—suffering with, for and because of oppressed people—incarnates the gospel of Christ, comes alive in people's hearts and minds. When this occurs, people are emboldened and change begins to take place.

At just such a point the Migrant Ministry, an authentic social change ministry, began showing some parallels between its theology and certain aspects of liberation theology. These similarities reflect not just an historical happenstance but rather how the wider church sought its own style for living out its mandate—"to do justice, to love kindness, and to walk humbly with your God" (Mi 6:8).

Both the little band of apostles following Jesus and the primitive church born at Pentecost discovered, as does each succeeding generation in the context of its peculiar need, that every theology that emerges is, of necessity, shaped by its historical context and its own development.

In many ways the ancients as well as the moderns have spoken to the same social situations and responded to the same rising expectations. Always it has been the desperate condition of the marginalized people of the society, when they have been exploited and oppressed by an entrenched ruling class, who are eventually forced to seek change and, in so doing, to call the church to act with them in their struggle for liberation. Thank God for the times the church has responded.

In liberation theology an essential factor consists of telling one's own story, and identifying as a people, as a community.

By uniting in the story of poverty and injustice and coming together in solidarity, people gain a new consciousness and a new strength to address their suffering. The masses of poor people living in the barrios and favelas of Latin American cities and in the labor camps and rural slums of agricultural California, experienced this powerful moving of the Spirit. A new people and a movement came into being.

A reinterpretation of the proclamation made at what many consider to be the birthplace of liberation theology—the historic Latin American Bishops Conference in Medellin, Colombia, 1968—highlights the oneness of farm workers and the Latin American poor. It said, "Latin America [farm workers] will undertake [their] liberation at the cost of whatever sacrifice, not in order to seal [themselves] off, but in order to open [themselves] to union with the rest of the world, giving and receiving in a spirit of solidarity."

It is a challenge for the church to be in solidarity with oppressed people in the United States or in Latin America. Out of this experience of solidarity, the church began to realize a profound truth—oppressed people understand clearly their own needs, can—given resources and a servanthood relationship with Christians—organize themselves for action in a sustained and thoughtful program leading to appropriate, fundamental change.

The American church, both north and south, learned that it is the oppressed people themselves who will achieve their own liberation. Thus the church must listen, become the servant of the oppressed and in that enabling role accept the leadership of the poor, offering the church's skills and resources to help where possible and make connections to other useful segments of society.

Several other common characteristics of the practice of liberation theology—praxis—emerged within the Migrant Ministry: 1). The process normally would begin with prayerful reflection, to be followed by action to relieve injustice, followed again by further reflection. 2). Social evil began to be perceived not just as residing in the individual, but rather as corporate and systemic in the way society functions, allowing for the enrichment of one group at the expense of another. 3). The absolute necessity to avoid the all-too-human attitudes of paternalism, sexism and condescension towards the poor which is held by many persons in power who quickly blame the victims for their own plight and thus rationalize their own participation in creating the conditions which oppress the poor. 4). A realistic view of the function of power in society.

Liberation theologians frequently used marxist analysis to understand and explain the great disparity between the relatively few rich people and the multitudinous lower class— predominant in Latin societies—thus locating the root cause of oppression in the struggle between these economic classes. On the other hand, while recognizing that agribusiness interests used their economic and political power to maintain their position of dominance in society, neither the Migrant Ministry nor the union leadership used marxist analysis as a tool in arriving at their understanding of the causes of poverty in America. Though Chavez was often accused by his detractors of communism, he was not marxist.

Perhaps the most significant similarity between the positions of liberation theologians and the theological assumptions of the Migrant Ministry lies in their common views regarding the need to realign power and change its locus. For both, their goal was to achieve justice for the powerless using the methods that would assist the poor to organize themselves and thus gain the power they could exert through the force of their own lives. "People Power" is the new cry for justice.

The civil rights movement in the United States benefited from rising expectations, especially in the black community, as Martin Luther King, Jr. appealed to the rising expectations of poor blacks as well as to the conscience of the American people when he called for a greater measure of justice for the poor.

This had a twofold effect because the hope of the poor was not taken away while on the other hand their determination to change their status was reinforced. For some middle class persons their conscience was touched to the degree that they moved to solidarity with the poor. A new alignment of power came about and change occurred.

A unique development in the Latin American experience of

liberation theology occurred among the rural poor in Brazil where communities of peasants met regularly with catechists—or coordinators of the community as they were called. These coordinators filled the vacuum caused by the absence of priests and in fact they were often nuns who were deemed unqualified for ordination to the priesthood by the church's hierarchy. The communities of people who came together in these meetings became known as *comunidades eclesiais de base* or basic church communities.

One example of how these developed is illustrated in the response of Dom Agnelo Rossi, the local bishop of the diocese of Barra do Pirai, to a complaint of a pious old lady, "In Natal the three Protestant churches are lit up and crowded. We hear their hymn-singing. . . and our Catholic church, closed, is in darkness . . . because we don't get a priest." The bishop's response was to make available catechists to such groups (Cook *The Expectation of the Poor* 1985:64). An estimated 100,000 of these communities exist today in Brazil involving over 3,500,000 persons.

Comparable grass roots movements have occurred throughout Latin America. A major force in the revolutionary movements in Nicaragua and other Central American countries comes from the support of the so-called popular church which emerged from the base communities there.

Among day-to-day activities, members engage in typing, sewing, dressmaking, carpentry, health and hygiene courses and leadership training. Religious instruction and clubs for mothers or young people also are included in the program. The communities promote cooperation and shared tasks, community volunteer work and social meetings. Perhaps the most important function involves regular meetings for discussion, Bible study, reflection and action. Where before the word of the ecclesial structure was accepted without question, today the people hear the word directly through scripture.

Small groups meet to read a Bible passage. The catechist gives a brief background of the passage which is read through two or three times. Then a discussion focuses on three questions: 1). What did Jesus do? (not what he said, but what he did) 2). Whom did Jesus help and how? and 3). Who opposed Jesus in doing these things? The answers are recorded then a second discussion is held with these questions: 1). Who is doing similiar deeds today? 2). Who is being helped by these Christlike actions? and 3). Who is in opposition today? The questions and answers reflect the life experiences of the people; the Biblical stories and their stories become one.

Although outwardly the Migrant Ministry and the United Farm Worker's union bear little resemblance to the base communities, they do deal in similar ways with issues affecting the lives of marginalized persons struggling to overcome oppression. The values sought—dignity, freedom and self-determination—though implicit in the American culture, have always been out of reach of farm workers just as their right to collective bargaining and unionization was denied.

Another similarity appears in the communitarian or communal form of the union which is demonstrated in the subsistence life-style adopted by all. This parallels the sacrifice of the people in basic church communities. The farm workers' willingness to sacrifice in order to establish their union, their unique form of organization and their very lives, provided a unifying and strengthening force to their movement. Further, in their call for justice for all, not just better conditions for themselves, they present a challenge to the whole of society.

In both of the major divisions of Christianity—Roman Catholic and Protestant—the theological thrust for social justice has had a long history. Coexisting in both faiths has been what may be called privatized religion. The more orthodox position, now often referred to as the "preferential option for the poor," never entirely lost out, yet it often was not fully accepted by the hierarchy and so was not able to be actualized in parish life or in many missionary and evangelistic programs.

Thus liberation theology emerged in South and Central America, both Catholic and Protestant, in the 1950s. At this time also the Migrant Ministry made its historic change in policy and ministry.

In its attempt to bring into praxis the Biblical imperative for justice for the poor, liberation theology asserts that the world should be Christianized through humanization, love, justice and self-determination. A tension has existed for centuries between orthodoxy and orthopraxy—between right-belief and right-action. The theology of the Migrant Ministry and the union sought to follow a proper balance between these two.

Liberation theology stresses praxis as crucial in the life of the people which, surely, the church has encouraged throughout history. In its efforts to proclaim the Biblical message it has sought, with varying success, to achieve a dynamic balance between faith and works and discovered in the process that often a people must undergo struggle and sacrifice before liberation is achieved. Before action can be effectively directed, an accurate analysis of society's goals and processes must be accomplished.

Farm workers have long known the different behaviours of individual small farmers and giant corporations. Working for a corporate farm means one will usually receive cold, impersonal treatment from managers who often see workers as commodities to be bought and sold. Working for an individual farmer, at least, feels like being part of a family. This comes nearer to their Latin mores.

14. Religious Community Support

From the early 1920s the Migrant Ministry, representing the cooperating Protestant churches of the country, had shown consistent support of farm workers and their poverty. Catholic and Jewish groups likewise had displayed concern with the desperate plight of farm workers. As the strike and related activities continued, the support of the faith community grew. The Catholic church, of course,˙ had a special role because of the religious heritage of the workers. A number of individual bishops, as well as the U.S. Catholic Conference of Bishops, were actively involved all along the way. Jewish bodies made their contributions to the struggle.

From the founding of the N.F.W.A., the Migrant Ministry committed itself to stand with Chavez and the farm workers in their David and Goliath challenge of the entrenched power of agribusiness and the financial community. As the strike and boycott expanded, the Migrant Ministry deployed itself to effectively undergird Chavez' bold effort, making available—through its connections with denominations, councils of churches, local churches and the general public—an effective and helpful communications network. Hartmire, Chavez and others appeared at regional and national judicatory meetings, seeking and getting active support—both moral and financial.

Of course the farm workers bore the main burden of the struggle, but the churches formed an effective support network. Hartmire and Chavez became skillful in arranging for prominent clergy and other church leaders to visit strike locations in order to verify the union's fidelity to its pledge of nonviolence. Often, when violence occurred, these visitors witnessed the event and

testified to its source. Their testimony that the violence was per-
petrated by the grower employees, or because of police brutality,
was effective in several instances, maintaining public confidence
in the justice of the cause.

Such groups often issued forceful statements which were
given wide attention. After their visit to Delano on December
14, 1965, eleven national church leaders released a statement
which said, among other things, "As clergy and laity of many
religious groups—Protestant, Roman Catholic and Jewish—we
came to Delano to inform ourselves at firsthand about the three-
month long strike of the grape pickers, (and the involvement of
religious bodies).

"The right of churches and synagogues to engage in such
action is absolutely clear to us. We reject the heresy that churches
and synagogues are to be concerned only with so-called 'spiritual'
matters. We believe that this is God's world which he not only
made but continues to love. Consequently, whatever goes on in
this world must be our concern, particularly when God's will for
the well-being of any of the children of God is being violated.

"We are not permitted to leave such considerations in the
arena of pious generalities. They must be specific, and for us
they have become burningly specific in the Delano grape strike.
We are not ignorant of the economic pressures on small farmers
and we expect the churches to stand with these farmers as change
is thrust upon them. But the suffering of farm workers and their
children cries to heaven and demands the attention of persons of
conscience.

"Farm workers are worthy. Their labor is important to the
agricultural industry. It is both natural and just that they should
participate in the decision-making process about wages, working
conditions and automation. Our three religious traditions have
long recognized this fact and repeatedly called for responsible
collective bargaining between employers and employees in all
industries. It is apparent to us that this basic right is being denied
to farm workers in this valley. Since this right to bargain with
strength as free [people] has been consistently denied to farm
workers their only recourse, in an effort to gain it for themselves,

has been to strike. We are satisfied that no other avenues of procedure have remained open to them. Consequently we feel compelled to identify ourselves unambiguously with their protest against such unjust treatment, and commend the pledge of nonviolence which they have faithfully fulfilled."

This statement went on to list seven specific recommendations for the churches, signed by four Catholic, one Jewish and six Protestant leaders. The statement was heeded by many in the churches and synagogues, if not by the growers and the government.

During this time, the 30 members of the state commission of the Migrant Ministry worked to build greater understanding of the strike among their constituencies. The members of the commission had been delegated by the denominations and other church groups like the United Church Women to provide a natural communication network between the migrants and the churches. The commission members organized many public meetings, wrote articles for church publications, gave speeches wherever an audience could be assembled and, most effectively of all, arranged trips to the strike areas for groups of clergy and laity.

A typical example of how this interpretive conduit worked in reaching the middle class communities involves commission consultant, Professor Henry Panian of Orange Coast College, Costa Mesa, California. After becoming involved in the farm worker movement he went back home and related his concerns to his pastor, Warren Studer. This resulted in a Thanksgiving offering being raised for the Migrant Ministry. Several other local churches responded to Panian's appeal. Commission members often joined the picket lines or met with growers and others in the farming areas in order to have a firsthand understanding of events.

During these visits the clergy, especially when they wore their clerical collars, served as an effective restraining presence, trying to minimize the violence shown by grower personnel and the sheriff's deputies. These firsthand experiences of the farm worker's plight by those who could readily articulate and could communicate to large groups of their own church members also reassured the farm workers that they were not alone in the struggle but had the urban people with them.

Not all such visitations went smoothly. From the beginning of the strike in September, pickets had been allowed freely to communicate with strikebreakers working in the fields. Communication took many forms—some displayed signs and posters urging the workers to come out of the fields, others shouted slogans across the fields, often by bullhorn, calling them out to join the *huelga*. Finally, during the week of October 10, the Kern County sheriff decided this kind of communication with strikebreakers was illegal. However, the sheriff of Tulare County disagreed and declined to join him in an action based on that interpretation of the law.

The conflict escalated on October 17 when Dave Havens, a staff person working with the T.C.C.D., was arrested on the charge of "disturbing the peace." His specific crime had been to read aloud Jack London's *Definition of a Strikebreaker*. Based on this novel interpretation of the law the sheriff also arrested, for "unlawful assembly," 44 persons including Chris Bergtholdt—a grower and a member of the state commission—Chris Hartmire and nine other ordained clergy.

The court failed to issue an injunction on a technicality, deeming that the accused persons had been assembled on public property lawfully. Charges were dismissed.

High-handed police activity such as this served to widen the gulf between those who supported the churches' stance and their critics. No amount of reasoned discourse could have more clearly shown the isolated, powerless position of the oppressed workers. Their isolation was demonstrated in that only labor and the church, in the main, stood with them in their pain and struggle. To most of society Chavez appeared, when noticed at all, a modern day Don Quixote, or worse.

Chris Hartmire remembers the urgency felt by the Migrant Ministry at that time. "The expectations of low-income people are revolutionary, not evolutionary. They want justice now and not special services for an unjust interim. Farm workers want to be organized so they can have power to change their situation."

The many historical attempts at union organization had ended when crushed by the power of growers. It would seem that the march of events defined the ministry in each time period. The vision for farm workers that Chavez and Hartmire held was, to some extent, shared by many of their predecessors who, sadly, failed in its realization. Analysis of the factors which made the farm worker movement succeed in the 1960s may well occupy our minds for a long time. The story we have told of the coming together of the faith community and the farm workers constitutes a great chapter in the never ending struggle, in this broken world, for justice for all persons. This history demonstrates the power and effectiveness of a committed, faithful response by God's people. Justice will be achieved only through such sacrificial commitment.

There is a profound lesson to be taken from this history of the single-minded devotion of the California Migrant Ministry, under Hartmire's leadership, to the farm worker worker movement. Committed women and men, allied in service with the poor, whose suffering stemmed from unjust economic and social structures, came to understand the call of God in the suffering of these same poor and responded in love. Through this interaction the Migrant Ministry and the union, together, jolted the middle class church out of its complacency, revealing the nature and power of its ministry with the oppressed, apparently powerless, people whose labor made possible our very life. We thank God that the church did not abandon its Migrant missionaries, and even when the going got rough, stood with them and the farm workers.

The struggle goes on.

Epilogue

Events: 1970 - 1986

This chronology of selected events illustrates the nature of the farm worker movement's continuing struggle with agribusiness. These economic and political forces arrayed against them show no signs of acceptance or accommodation.

1970—Contracts signed by 140 grape growers with the United Farm Workers as a result of the first grape boycott.

As soon as the grape contracts are signed, the lettuce growers call in the Teamsters and sign sweetheart contracts.

U.F.W. calls a boycott of head lettuce.

1971—The U.F.W., through a massive letter writing campaign, defeats a Republican effort to bring farm workers under the National Labor Relations Act.

1972—Farm workers defeat Proposition 22, a repressive collective bargaining act on the California ballot.

1973—The grape contracts expire and again the grape growers sign sweetheart deals with the Teamsters Union.

The U.F.W. calls second grape boycott.

1974—U.F.W. calls a boycott of Gallo wines.

1975—Pressure from the boycott succeeds in persuading agribusiness to agree to the passage of the Agricultural Labor Relations Act (A.L.R.A.).

1976—The A.L.R.A. is out of funds within nine months. The U.F.W. qualifies Proposition 14 for the California ballot which would have made the budget of the A.L.R.A. part of the state constitution. That effort failed.

1976-1977—Church people conduct field surveys and do lobbying in Sacramento to insure that the law is working after new funding is given.

1975-1980—Over 500 elections are held in the fields of California, the great majority being won by the U.F.W.

1975-1982—A variety of smaller, short boycotts are conducted to insure farm workers' election victories result in contracts, as required by the new law: Ralston Purina, Chaquita Bananas, Dole Bananas.

1979—The largest strike of lettuce workers occurs in the Coachella and Salinas Vallies. Rufino Contreras is killed. U.F.W. calls a boycott of Red Coach lettuce. Secondary boycott of Lucky-Gemco.

The Farm Labor Organizing Committee (F.L.O.C.) of the Midwest launches a boycott of Campbell Soup Company products.

1982—George Deukmejian is elected governor of California with major campaign funding from agribusiness interests.

1983—Deukmejian appoints David Stirling general counsel of the A.L.R.B. and the law begins to be used against farm worker organizing rights.

1984—The U.F.W. realizes the A.L.R.A. is not working and calls a new table grape boycott.

1986—F.L.O.C. wins contracts in the Ohio and Michigan tomato fields with growers contracting with the Campbells' Soup Company.

Friends of the National Farm Worker Ministry

The National Farm Worker Ministry staff is grateful to the following friends whose contributions have made this publication possible and whose faithful support has been greatly appreciated down through the years.

Yvonne Alcala
Dorothy J. Alexander
All Saints Episcopal Church, Pasadena, CA
American Friends Service Committee, Pasadena, CA
Rev. William J. Amundsen
Janet C. Anderson
Lee Anderson
Anonymous
Ann Appley
Walter & Edna Armantage
John Armendariz
Kathreen Arscott
Rabbi Haim Asa
Rev. & Mrs. Sadaichi Asai
Association of Chicago Priests, IL
William D. & Ruth L. Auld
Tom Auxter
Harold & Martha Bakke
Elizabeth Burnham Baldwin
Alice Barnes
Mrs. Lucille M. Bates
Donna Bedau
Fanda Bender & Sheila Gam
John C. Bennett
Carylon & Al Berry
Fred B. Blair
John C. Blair
June Blair
David & Anne Blankenhorn

Barbara Ann Blessing
Roger & Mary Boyvey
Tom & Patricia Brown
Arthur Brunwasser
John & Eleanor Buchanan
David & Ginny Burnight
Clarence V. Caldwell
Capuchin Missions, Province of St. Joseph
Mr. and Mrs. Fortino Mike Cardenas
Laura Carpenter
Centro Cristo Rey—Spanish Speaking Apostolate, Rockford, IL
Barbara F. Cernohlavek
James W. Cernohlavek
Eleanor & Bill Chandler, Sr.
Flora Chavez
Dixie Lee Chavez-Irvin
Ken Childs
Church Women United in Central Pinellas Co., FL
Church Women United in Upper Pinellas Co., FL
Church Women United, Wisconsin, Executive Board
Donald B. Clark
Henry B. Clark II
Jan & John Simpson Clement
Gordon Clint
Andy Coe
Faith A. Sand & Albert G. Cohen

Coleccion Tloque Nahuaque, U. of
  California, Santa Barbara
Rev. Ann Marie Coleman
Rev. Donald Coleman
Gary Commins
Rabbi Ernst J. Conrad
Dolores A. Conroy
Avelina & Robert Coriell
Council of Religious, Diocese of
  Brownsville, TX
Covenant Presbyterian Church,
  Los Angeles, CA
Mrs. Frederick W. Cropp
John P. Crossley, Jr.
Daughters of Mary and Joseph
Nathan & Edith Davis
A. Garnett Day
Bishop Jesse R. DeWitt
Fr. Daniel Derry
Rev. William Dew, Jr.
Rev. J. W. (Bill) Dillinger
Rev. Terence L. Dosh, Ph.D.
Pearl Doughty
Bill Lane Doulos
Dorothy Drummond
Pete T. Duarte
Charles W. Dubs
Mary Judith Dunbar
M. Frances Dyer
Fern M. Ebertz
Miriam Eisler
Hermana Caremlita Espinoza
Fr. Martin Farrell
Gwen Felton
Mr. & Mrs. Ray T. Ferguson
Dr. Harold E. Fey
Caroline Fischer
Rev. John D. Fischer
Lynne S. Fitch
Sandra Squire Fluck
Monsignor James B. Flynn
The Rt. Rev. William H. Folwell

Hugo & Tommi Francis
Franciscan Sisters of the Poor,
  Brooklyn, NY
Norman C. Frank
Mary Murphy Freedlund
Fr. Ed Fronske, o.f.m.
Margaret A. Faud
Luci Arellano Gajec
Patricia & Stephen Gallagher
Hector Garcia
Bishop Oliver B. Garver, Jr.
Eileen R. Gavel
Ellen Geer
Samuel Gendelman
Dan & Frances Genung
Alla Belle C. Gest
Dr. Ray Gibbons
Marjorie Hartmire Gifford
Jeanne & Roy Giordano
Rabbi Joseph B. Glaser
Alice O. Glasser
Kay M. Goffer
Ruth Weisman Goldboss
Rabbi Jerrold Goldstein
Bernice M. Gordon
Outreach Committee,
  Grace Episcopal Church,
  Mt. Glemens, MI
Green Library, Stanford University,
  CA
Guadalupe Social Services,
  Immokalee, FL
Mary A. Guillen
Rev. Patricio Guillen
Amador A. Gutierrez
Rev. & Mrs. John H. Hager
Captain Lyle E. Hall
Margaret Halliwell
Don Hancock
Margaret Jessup Hanson
Jay & Elsie Harber
Arthur E. Harrington

Chris & Jane Hartmire
Margarert Hathaway
Liz & Chuck Henser
Albert L. Hernandez
Rev. J. A. Hernandez
Lydia Hernandez
The Herndon Family
Frederick & Kristin Herzog
Rev. Msgr. George C. Higgins
Pamela Higgins
Joy Hintz
Mr. and Mrs. John G. Hoepfl
Dr. and Mrs. Cecil Hoffman
Genie Holmes
James J. Horgan
Dr. Joseph P. Hough
Sara E. Wilson & Gustavo C.
   Houghton
Jean Powers Howard
Karen Kumari Hudson-Bates
Mrs. Edward J. Hummel Jr.
Mr. and Mrs. Edward J. Hustoles
Local Lodge 2319, IAMAW,
   Tampa, FL
India Foundation
Karl & Ethelyn Irvin
Paul Jacobs
Rabbi Dr. Sidney J. Jacobs
Shirley B. James
Sr. Carol Frances Jegen, BVM
Lawrence J. Jelinek
Bab Agnes Jenkins
Dr. Bruce Jessup
George & Linda Johnson
Clifford & Rosa Julstrom
Evelyn Keast
Fred Keast
Julian & Jeanette Keiser
Michael A. Kelly
Ralph & Nat Kennedy
Robert Francis Kennedy
Rev. Kenneth Kennon

Mary Ellen Kennon
Ernest H. King
Ellen M. Kinney
Rev. Dr. Dwight L. Kintner
Clarrissa L. Kitchen
Janet Vandevender & Paul Kittlaus
Fiona Knox
Bishop & Mrs. J. Lloyd Knox
A. V. Krebs
Elizabeth LaForest, R.S.M.
Eileen & Paul LeFort
John Michael Lee, Esq.
Fr. Bill Leininger
Karen Lepper
Velma Lerned
Florence Lerrigo
Rev. Harold Letts
Mrs. Isabel Letts
Cricket Levering
Jean E. Lewis
Rabbi Albert M. Lewis, D.D.
Jessie Linares
Anne Loftis
Los Angeles Catholic Worker
William Love
Howell & Jean Lowe
Edith M. Lowry
Frank C. Mabee
John MacLaughlin
Sandra MacLaughlin
Shirley Magidson
Bill Maher
Marilyn & Richard Mandel
Pamela & Bob Mang
Barbara Manley
Mrs. Sonya Manrriquez
Bob Marshall
Phillip P. Mason
Carl N. Mather, Jr.
Fr. John Maxwell
Jean S. Maynard
Lester G. McAllister

Margaret Ann & Myles McCabe
Miss Beatrice McConnell
Gene McCornack
William & Barbara McCoy
Marian & Murray McDougal
Mary C. McFarland
Kilian McGown, C.P.
The Rev. Charles C. McLain
Roberta, Jim, Maria, Alain &
  Mark McLaughlin
Regina S. Meissner
Irene D. Mendez
Carol Anne Messina, S.C.N.
Edward W. Meury
Michigan Farm Worker Ministry
  Coalition
Midwest Migrant Health
  Information Office
Andrew S. Miller
Tom Miller
Milwaukee Archdiocesan Sisters
  Council
Sue Miner
Mary & Ed Mirch
James H. Moore
Barbara A. Moote
John J. Moran
Susan Yarrow Morris
Nelle Morton
Helen Moser
Mildred Moser
Anne Napier Mott
Leo & Jane Mutchler
Patricia-Egan & Charles K. Myers
John Napier
Joy Napier
John A. Nasstrom
L. J. Nelson, Jr.
Tom & Grace Nelson
Virginia & Charles Nesmith
Fr. Dick Notter
Laurel & Abe Ohanian

John & Sylvia Oleck
Fr. Silas Oleksinski, OFM
Kent M. Organ
Jane Hanna Oseid
Rev. Frederick George Overdier
Henry & Barbara Panian
Margaret Ekstrom Paul
Fr. Jose Pawlicki
Mrs. Eric C. Pepys
Martha B. Petersen
Floy L. Peterson
John W. Peterson
Rev. Cletus Henry Pfab, S.J.
Lucky Phelps
Nancy Phelps
Christie Miles Phillips
Cruz E. Phillips
Pilgrim Place Library
Joseph Podorsek
Adele Pollard
Gary F. Potwin
Walter S. Press
Bernice Ranford
Robert & Martha Rankin
Dr. William W. Rankin
Helen Sue Read
Lynne Reade, Attorney at Law
Redemptorist Societies of the West
Redemptorist Affiliates in Kansas
Lucie S. Reedy
Dr. George F. Regas
Jon L. Regier
Fred P. Register
Rev. John L. Reid
Joel Rentz
Marietta N. Reynolds
Jose Rios & Marie Palacios-Rios
Francisca Rivas
Elizabeth Robinson
Gilberto Robledo
Domingo Rodriguez
Tony Rodriguez

Fred Roesti
Don & Kay Rogers
Gustavo Romero
Nina Rosenberg-Yardeini
Josiah V. Roth
Charles & Peggy Rymes
SEPI Bookstore
Nancy & Tim Sampson
Olgha Sierra Sandman
Carmen Sarati, SSJ
Mary Sawyer
Joel Schaffer
Mr. and Mrs. Farrel L. Schell
David Schilling
William & June Scholes
Marti & Richard Schrank
Mr. & Mrs. Charles A. Scott Sr.
D. Lee & Ruth Scott
Therese Voorhis Scott
Harvey Seifert
Casto C. Serna
Edward S. Setchko
Jewell & Kathleen Sexton
Harry E. Shaner
Berta Silva
Consuelo & Carolos Simental
R. Wilbur Simmons
Sisters of St. Francis, Philadelphia,
    PA
Sisters of St. Francis of Assisi,
    Milwaukee, WI
Sisters of St. Francis, Mission, TX
Sisters of St. Joseph of Orange, CA
Sisters, Servants of the Immaculate
    Heart of Mary, Mission Province
Sisters, Servants of the Immaculate
    Heart of Mary, Monroe, MI
Barb & Ken Smith
St. Martin De Porres Parish,
    Warren, MI
St. Patrick Church, Union Lake, MI
St. Scholastic Convent Library

St. Sylvester Christian Service
The Rev. John F. Stevens
Rev. Jerald Stinson
Patricia Stockton
Dr. & Mrs. John B. Streater
Rev. Sharon Streater
John C. Stuhr
Virginia A. Stuhr
Ruth Sugerman
Norman W. Taylor
Scott R. Templeton
Jim Terry
Nate Thornton
Joe Tobin
Perfecta Toledo
Bette Traynor
Matthew James Trickey
Phillip John Trickey
Dr. Samuel B. Trickey
Marijane Trodella
Mary S. Tuller
Carrie M. Turk
Christine L. Turk
Jack & Diane Turk
Gary Tutunjian
Fred Tymeson
Maggie Tyson
Samuel R. Tyson
Wallace & Carol Umber
United Food & Commercial Workers
    Union, Local 428, AFL-CIO
Rev. Benjamin J. Urmston, S.J.
Carolyn Vallerga
Dale Van Pelt
Jan Van Pelt
Gladys Verhulst
WILPF—Bucks County Chapter
Colette Walker
Hal M. Warheim
Mrs. Sarah Hulshoff Waszink
Rev. J. Will Wauters
Sally Weinland

Virginia Weitlauf
Gertrude Welch
John & Hazel White
Rev. John K. White
Pearl White
Dick Wiesenhahn
Charles C. Williams
Gordon H. & Felicia J. Williamson
Anthony G. Wilson
Lorraine Wilson
Peter & Martha Wilson
Virginia A. Wilson
Frances Winter
Audrey Witte
Bee R. Wolfe
Judge & Mrs. Delbert Wong
Virginia B. Wyatt
Lydia C. Wyatt
Marjorie A. Yingst
George D. & Doris Anne Younger
Sylvia Zamarripa
Sister Rosa Martha Zaratę, SJS
Betty Poteet Zimmerman
Willard J. Zinn, M.D.